FEMINISM IS QUEER

About the Author

Mimi Marinucci completed a PhD in philosophy and a graduate certificate in women's studies from Temple University in 2000. Currently serving as associate professor of philosophy and women's and gender studies at Eastern Washington University, Marinucci teaches courses on feminism, philosophy, and feminist philosophy. Marinucci, who is especially interested in the subjective and social aspects of knowledge production, particularly knowledge produced around issues of gender and sexuality, is the author of several articles that employ references from popular culture in the service of a more scholarly agenda. Examples include 'There's Something Queer About The Onion' (forthcoming in *The Onion and Philosophy*, edited by Sharon Kaye), 'What's Wrong with Porn?' (in *Porn – Philosophy for Everyone: How to Think with Kink*, edited by Dave Monroe), 'Television, Generation X, and Third Wave Feminism: A Contextual Analysis of the Brady Bunch' (*Journal of Popular Culture*, Volume 38, Number 3, February 2005), and 'Feminism and the Ethics of Violence: Why Buffy Kicks Ass' (in *Buffy the Vampire Slayer and Philosophy: Fear and Trembling in Sunnydale*, edited by James B. South). Marinucci is also the founding editor of *Wave 2.5: A Feminist Zine*, a two-time Utne Independent Press Award nominee (2005, 2009).

FEMINISM IS QUEER

The intimate connection between queer and feminist theory

MIMI MARINUCCI

Zed Books
London & New York

Feminism is Queer: The intimate connection between queer and feminist theory was first published in 2010 by Zed Books Ltd, 7 Cynthia Street, London N1 9JF, UK and Room 400, 175 Fifth Avenue, New York, NY 10010, USA

www.zedbooks.co.uk

Typeset in Sabon by Free Range Book Design & Production Limited
Cover designed by www.alice-marwick.co.uk
Printed and bound by Mimeo Ltd, Huntingdon, Cambridgeshire, PE29 6XX.

MIX
Paper from
responsible sources
FSC
www.fsc.org   FSC® C019549

Distributed in the USA exclusively by Palgrave Macmillan, a division of St Martin's Press, LLC, 175 Fifth Avenue, New York, NY 10010, USA

A catalogue record for this book is available from the British Library
Library of Congress Cataloging in Publication Data available

ISBN 978 1 84813 474 4 hb
ISBN 978 1 84813 475 1 pb
ISBN 978 1 84813 476 8 eb

Contents

Figures

Acknowledgements

Throughout my life, I have benefited from the unwavering support of my parents, Sam Marinucci and Jan Marinucci, as well as my siblings, Robynn Schlup, Ev Marinucci, and John Marinucci. My family fostered my lifelong love affair with school, as did a number of excellent teachers, notably Ken Edwards, now retired from W. Reily Brown Elementary School, and Linda Gehling, now retired from Caesar Rodney High School. Years later, as a graduate student at Temple University, where I began developing some of the ideas presented in this book, I was encouraged by Miriam Solomon and Chuck Dyke of Temple University, as well as Sandra Harding, who was then teaching for part of each year at the University of Delaware. I didn't realize it at the time, but I was forever changed when Sandra Harding first introduced me to queer theory.

I am extremely grateful for ongoing encouragement and support from the staff and faculty of the EWU Women's and Gender Studies programme, including Christi Wavada, Carol Vines, Kelly Coogan and, especially, Sally Winkle and Elizabeth Kissling, who have provided much-needed mentoring throughout my career at EWU. I am also grateful for the members of the EWU philosophy programme, particularly Terry MacMullan, Kevin Decker, and Chris Kirby. These colleagues are some of my favourite people, and I am better for knowing them. I have also benefited from the ongoing exchange of ideas with faculty across disciplinary boundaries. I would like to thank Jenny Thomson for organizing monthly gatherings of women faculty and staff to share Thai food and discuss our ongoing projects and research, including portions of this book. I would also like to thank the members of the EWU College of Social and Behavioral Sciences 'Theory Committee' for many discussions about the philosophy of the social sciences. Finally, I would like to thank Gary Krug for advice about the academic publishing process and about transforming my fledgling ideas into a *bona fide* prospectus.

Special thanks go to my friends and colleagues of the American Association of Philosophy Teachers for helping me to develop my understanding of who I am as a teacher, a philosopher, and a person, and also for helping me to develop my understanding of teaching philosophy and doing philosophy as complementary practices, rather than competing or conflicting activities. Indeed, while much of the work for this project was done during a 2007–2008 sabbatical from teaching, generously funded by Eastern Washington University, most of it was done in direct connection with my teaching. I have benefited from discussions with students in many of my classes, most notably 'GLBT Studies' and, more recently, 'Queer Theory', which I offered for the first time in the spring quarter of 2010. The students in this course graciously read the chapters of this manuscript, occasionally as unedited first drafts, providing formative feedback and welcome encouragement along the way. Over the past several years, many students, including some I now count among my friends and colleagues, have contributed substantially to my understanding of gender, sex, and sexuality. One such example is Kenny Capps, who served as a teaching assistant for my 'GLBT Studies' course in the fall quarter of 2006. Others include Megan Cuilla, Sali McNamee (now Sayler), and Kimberly Stankovich, with whom I collaborated on a 'Constructed Identities' panel for the Queer ID Conference at Boise State University in October 2006. I am also grateful for conversations, some more recent than others, with Michael Barrett, Willow Moline, Krista Benson, and countless others.

Before I even knew what it meant, my friend Jeff Thorpe accused me of being a philosopher. Almost thirty years later, I now understand how remarkable it was, first, that someone knew me well enough to accurately project the trajectory of my adult life and, second, that I had a friend who liked me because of, rather than in spite of, my penchant for analysis and deconstruction. I am fortunate to have the support of a few other equally remarkable friends, including Jeff Wootten, Kim Rosenthal Budner, and Polly Buckingham. Polly Buckingham also deserves special thanks for teaching me that the surest way to get my work published is to submit my work for publication.

My personal life became complicated during the final stages of preparing this manuscript, and I will always be grateful to Heather Elder, Cameron Smith Norton, Cindy Wells, Tom Tam, and Jim Jenkins for reaching out to me with friendship in exactly the right ways at exactly the right times. I am also grateful to Carol Bjork and the other instructors and dancers at the Jazzercise Fitness Center of Spokane for helping me to maintain my physical and mental health through challenging times.

Finally, I would like to thank the editorial staff at Zed Books, particularly Tamsine O'Riordan, as well as the art team that designed the cover image, and an anonymous reader who provided useful suggestions for fine-tuning the final draft of this manuscript.

When the adventurers reassembled upon the roof it was found that a remarkably queer assortment of articles had been selected by the various members of the party. No one seemed to have a very clear idea of what was required, but all had brought something.

(L. Frank Baum, *The Marvelous Land of Oz*, p.67)

Preface

Not Just the New 'Gay'

It was a queerly assorted company, indeed, for there are more quaint and unusual characters in Oz than in all the rest of the world, and Ozma was more interested in unusual people than in ordinary ones – just as you and I are.

(L. Frank Baum, *The Magic of Oz*, p.568)

Once considered quite offensive, 'queer' is now used with increasing regularity, often as a straightforward alternative to 'gay'. Consider, for example, its use in the title of the recent HBO hit *Queer as Folk*, which featured a group of friends comprised mostly of gay-identified men, or Bravo's *Queer Eye for the Straight Guy* (later just *Queer Eye*), which featured fashion and lifestyle advice from, again, a group of gay-identified men. While I am neither naive enough nor arrogant enough to suppose that 'queer' admits of just one interpretation, namely the one I happen to provide, I do recognize that the casual trend of replacing 'gay' with 'queer' ignores some important theoretical work aimed at exposing the representational limitations of 'gay' and the comparable representational richness of 'queer'. I also recognize that the oversimplification of complicated concepts in the popular media is a sure sign that the larger culture is at least vaguely aware of those concepts. This book aims to provide background and context for those who are curious about the recent insertion of 'queer' into polite vernacular. This book also aims to provide background and context for those who encounter 'queer' in scholarly writing that is often so mired in technical jargon that it may seem utterly meaningless to the uninitiated.

Introductory texts in gender studies, sometimes identified as women's studies or feminist studies, address gender identity. Introductory texts in sexuality studies, sometimes identified as lesbian, gay, bisexual, and transgender studies (or LGBT studies), address sexual identity. Unfortunately, however, introductory texts situated at the intersection of gender identity and sexual identity are rare. This book is, in part, an attempt to fill that gap, and could therefore serve as a text for any course of study, be it in a university setting or in the context of independent scholarship, directed towards the examination of virtually any aspect of gender, sex, and sexuality.

The structure of this book makes it useful for readers at different levels and from different fields. While the chapters and sections of this book fit together as interconnected components of a coherent whole, they can also be read separately. Those who choose to read chapters or sections out of context or out of order should refer to the appendix as needed. Potentially unfamiliar terminology is carefully explained, often in footnotes, as it occurs throughout the text, and these explanations are in turn collected in the appendix, which is aptly titled 'Terms and Concepts'. This manner of presentation allows readers who do not require additional background information to read the main text with minimal interruption, while simultaneously offering helpful explication for those who need it. This is especially useful given that one of the greatest challenges in teaching queer theory, which is inherently interdisciplinary, is the varying degree of student familiarity with relevant background concepts. This often leads students to seek definitions, either from a dictionary or from the instructor. Unfortunately, dictionary definitions, which are detached from the specific context in which the terms occur, often do very little to promote understanding of specialized academic terminology. Indeed, queer theory resists the reductionist practice of pretending that it is possible to delineate, once and for all, the necessary and sufficient conditions for membership in any given category. Nevertheless, it is often necessary to provide an entering wedge for the uninitiated. Presenting contextualized explanations in the form of commentary and discussion provides this entering wedge without thereby pretending to offer a fixed or final account of that which is always and inevitably in a state of flux.

The book is divided into three main sections and a shorter fourth section. The first section, 'Sexuality', consists of three chapters, including Chapter 1, 'The Social Construction of Sexuality'; Chapter 2, 'The Social History of Lesbian and Gay Identity'; and Chapter 3, 'Queer Alternatives'. Chapter 1 summarizes the emergence of the various concepts of sexuality and sexual identity that exist in contemporary western culture, and compares them with concepts employed throughout history and across cultures. Chapter 2 traces the relatively recent emergence, first of gay identity, and then of lesbian identity. Chapter 3 then introduces queer identity as an alternative to more familiar categories of sexual identity, which usually concentrate on sexual partner choice and ignore the many other subtleties surrounding sexual pleasure and desire. The second section, 'Sex', consists of Chapter 4, 'Unwelcome Interventions', and Chapter 5, 'Welcome Transformations'. While Chapter 4 examines the role of medical technology in enforcing a boundary between female and male bodies, particularly in the case of intersex bodies, Chapter 5 explores the implications of this boundary enforcement for transgender people. The third section, 'Gender', consists of Chapter 6, 'Gender Defined and Undefined', and Chapter 7, 'Feminism Examined and Explored'. Chapter 6 examines the concept of gender, especially its role in linguistic contexts. Chapter 7 summarizes the various attitudes concerning gender and gender oppression collected under the banner of feminism. The fourth and final section, 'Queer Feminism', contains just one chapter, namely Chapter 8, titled 'Notes Toward a Queer Feminism', which explores what a queer approach to feminism might involve. I should note that although it is useful as a rough and ready way of organizing a potentially overwhelming body of material, the division of this material into sections on sexuality, sex, and gender is rather imprecise given the intimate interconnections between and among these concepts.

For those seeking only a brief introduction to queer theory, feminism, or the connections between them, this book, or even individual sections or chapters of this book, may be sufficient. For those seeking a more detailed explanation of these ideas and issues, each chapter provides a list of additional resources, including scholarly books and articles, as well as audio-visual material and works of fiction. Instead of recommending obscure material that the average reader would be unable to access, I have made an effort, whenever possible, to recommend material that is fairly easy to come by, for example in online sources or widely reprinted in various anthologies. I have included videos and novels for the dual purpose of providing relevant information and examples, while simultaneously implementing my understanding that people are sometimes better able to learn new material when it is presented in a variety of different formats.

I did not cover all of the material that I could have, and my decisions about what to include and what to exclude are largely the product of my own introduction to this literature. 'It is a delusion', notes Sandra Harding, 'to think that human thought could completely erase the fingerprints that reveal its production process' (Harding, 1993, p.57). This is the case with the representation of any subject matter, and therefore it is likewise the case, not only with queer theory and feminist theory in general, but also with my own representation of queer theory and feminist theory in particular. Although queer theory and feminist theory are both informed by lived experience and grass-roots activism, much of their development has taken place inside the ivory towers of academia. Insofar as queer theory and feminist theory constitute academic projects, they are inevitably covered with the fingerprints of race and class privilege. My presentation of this subject matter is no exception, reflecting the conditions of race and class privilege that characterize my experience as a white, middle-class, US woman with a PhD in philosophy and the security of a tenured university professorship.

Although I do not delve deeply into issues of race and class, this does not mean that queer theory and feminist theory have no bearing on issues of race and class, nor does it mean that issues of race and class have no bearing on queer theory and feminist theory. As discussed in Chapter 8, much of the appeal of queer theory and at least some forms of feminist theory is that, while ostensibly about gender, sex, and sexuality, they likewise comprise a critique of what Karen Warren (2000) refers to as the 'logic of domination', which attempts to justify the systematic subordination of those who lack power by those who possess it. Queer theory and feminist theory thus invite a critical analysis of racism, capitalism, globalization, and other expressions of the logic of domination. To the extent that a critical analysis of racism, capitalism, globalization, or anything else, can contribute to an understanding of the logic of domination, it thereby contributes to both queer theory and feminist theory.

Subtle but powerful expressions of the logic of domination are prevalent in the ordinary use of the English language, but I have taken care throughout this text to avoid unnecessarily oppressive turns of phrase. I resist what is sometimes referred to as ableist language, for example, by avoiding visual and auditory metaphors such as 'seeing' the point and 'listening' to reason. Instead, I reserve visual and auditory references for those fairly rare contexts in which vision or hearing is actually relevant to the ideas that I aim to express. This is analogous to avoiding allegedly generic uses of 'man' and 'men', as discussed in Chapter 6, and instead reserving those terms for contexts in which sex and gender are of some relevance. I also avoid the use of unnecessary bodily metaphors, such as 'standing up' for a cause. In addition, I resist the use of binary language by avoiding the gender pronouns 'he', 'she', 'him', 'his', and 'her', and I resist the use of universalizing language by avoiding the plural pronouns 'we' and 'our'. I also resist oppositional language by avoiding such expressions as 'arguably', and 'on the contrary'.

Throughout this book, I have attempted to avoid what Janice Moulton (1996) refers to as the adversary paradigm.

> Under the Adversary Paradigm, it is assumed that the only, or at any rate, the best, way of evaluating work in philosophy is to subject it to the strongest or most extreme opposition. And it is assumed that the best way of presenting work in philosophy is to address it to an imagined opponent and muster all the evidence one can to support it.
>
> (Moulton, 1996, p.14)

I therefore avoid the customary practice of offering premises in support of a clearly articulated conclusion, and then defending that conclusion by arguing against any concerns my opponents, real or imagined, would be likely to raise. Insofar as this manner of presentation disrupts the presumably stable meaning of what philosophical reasoning entails, it can be understood as an example of *queering*. This will be discussed in more detail later, but for now I will borrow from Krista Benson (2010) the delightfully simple explanation that queer theory is the recognition that 'shit's complicated'. Queering thus refers to the process of complicating something, and it is not necessarily limited to sexual contexts. Indeed, it is queer to do philosophy without making arguments. It is likewise queer to live in ways that challenge deeply held assumptions about gender, sex, and sexuality. Thus, queer encompasses even those who do not identify as homosexual (or even as lesbian, gay, bisexual, or transgender), but find that we are nevertheless incapable of occupying the compact spaces to which our cultural prescriptions regarding gender, sex, and sexuality have assigned us.

My interest in queering the philosophical process notwithstanding, I also aim to produce work that is both academically rigorous and philosophically significant. Toward this end, I have provided information that I take to be relevant in establishing context and background that will, hopefully, help readers understand how I arrived at a position I characterize in Chapter 8 as queer feminism. Because queer feminism supports the simultaneous viability of multiple forms of feminism, however, I have found it unnecessary to defend this form of feminism against other forms of feminism. While I could have geared my discussion toward an imaginary opponent who does not accept the legitimacy of any form of feminism, I opted instead to address my comments to the people I believe to be my likeliest readers: namely, those with an existing interest in theories of gender, sex, and sexuality.

References

Baum, L. F. (2005). *15 books in 1: L. Frank Baum's Original 'Oz' Series*. Shoes and Ships and Sealing Wax, Ltd. (Original works published 1908–20).

Benson, K. (2010). Personal communication.

Harding, S. (1993). 'Rethinking standpoint epistemology: What is "strong" objectivity?' In L. Alcoff and E. Potter (eds). *Feminist Epistemologies* (pp.49–82). New York: Routledge.

Moulton, J. (1996). 'A paradigm of philosophy: The adversary method'. In A. Garry and M. Pearsall (eds). *Women, Knowledge, and Reality: Explorations in Feminist Philosophy* (2nd ed.). New York: Routledge.

Warren, K. J. (2000). *Ecofeminist Philosophy: A Western Perspective on What It Is and Why It Matters*. Lanham, MD: Rowman & Littlefield.

SECTION I

SEXUALITY

'Dear me! Aren't you feeling a little queer, just now?'
Dorothy asked the Patchwork Girl.

(L. Frank Baum, *The Patchwork Girl of Oz*, p.295)

1

The Social Construction
of Sexuality

*'You're likely to see many queer things in the Land of Oz, sir,' said
the Wizard. 'But a fairy country is extremely interesting when you
get used to being surprised.'*
(L. Frank Baum, *The Emerald City of Oz*, p.219)

The Kinsey Report

Many people who support the interests of lesbian women and gay men
maintain that homosexuality is a universal phenomenon. Drawing
on research conducted by Alfred Kinsey and the Kinsey Institute,
homosexuality is often estimated to occur in roughly 10 per cent of the
population. Based on thousands of detailed interviews, Kinsey's findings
were published in two volumes: *Sexual Behavior in the Human Male*
(Kinsey, Pomeroy, and Martin, 1948) and *Sexual Behavior in the Human
Female* (Kinsey, Pomeroy, Martin, and Gebhard, 1953). These are often
referred to informally as the 'Kinsey Reports'. The Kinsey Reports
challenged conservative beliefs about sexuality by suggesting that taboo
practices, such as masturbation, promiscuity, and homosexuality, were
much more prevalent than previously acknowledged.

For better or worse, the oft-quoted statistic that homosexuality occurs
at a steady rate of 10 per cent is not a straightforward conclusion of the
Kinsey Reports. Kinsey actually reported that '37% of males and 13% of
females had at least some overt homosexual experience to orgasm' and
that '10% of males were more or less exclusively homosexual and 8%
of males were exclusively homosexual for at least three years between
the ages of 16 and 55'. Kinsey also reported 'a range of 2–6% for more
or less exclusively homosexual experience/response' among women.
Finally, it was reported that '4% of males and 1–3% of females had been
exclusively homosexual after the onset of adolescence up to the time of
the interview' (as cited by The Kinsey Institute, n.d.). If these figures

reveal anything about the rate of homosexuality, it would seem to be
that it is largely dependent on the method of accounting. Furthermore,
while Kinsey's subject pool was quite large, it was comprised primarily of
white college students in the Midwestern USA. The rate of homosexuality
within that demographic during the first half of the 20th century does not
necessarily generalize to other populations.

Kinsey's 'Hetero–Homosexual Rating Scale', referred to informally as
the 'Kinsey Scale', is often upheld as evidence that both bisexuality and
homosexuality are natural alternatives to heterosexuality.[1] The Kinsey
Scale classifies sexual orientation along seven categories numbered 0
through 6, with 0 representing those whose experiences and interests are
'exclusively heterosexual' and 6 representing those whose experiences
and interests are 'exclusively homosexual' (Kinsey *et al.*, 1948, p.638).
According to the Kinsey Scale, everyone else has at least some tendency
toward both homosexual and heterosexual expression (refer to Figure
1.1). Rejecting 'the assumption that homosexuality and heterosexuality
are two mutually exclusive phenomena' (Kinsey, 1941, p.425), Kinsey
avoided using 'homosexual' as a noun and instead referred adjectivally
to homosexual behaviours and attractions.

Figure 1.1 Kinsey's hetero–homosexual rating scale

Heterosexual–Homosexual Rating Scale

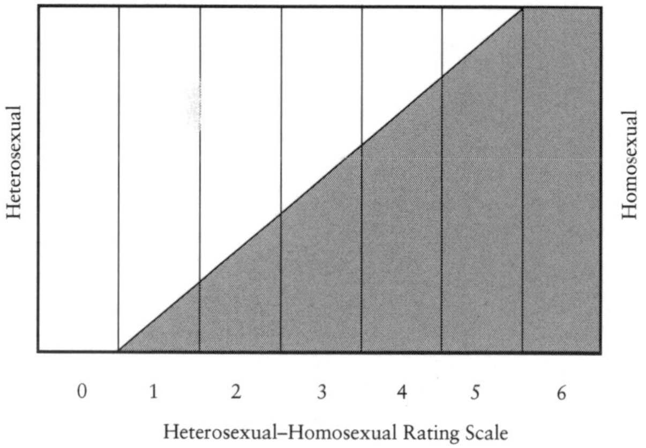

0   Exclusively heterosexual with no homosexual
1   Predominantly heterosexual, only incidentally homosexual
2   Predominantly heterosexual, but more than incidentally homosexual
3   Equally heterosexual and homosexual
4   Predominantly homosexual, but more than incidentally heterosexual
5   Predominantly homosexual, only incidentally heterosexual
6   Exclusively homosexual

Source: Kinsey, *et al.*, 1948, p.638 (as published online by the
Kinsey Institute, 1999)

Kinsey encouraged social awareness and acceptance of sexual diversity, but not by attempting to establish the universal existence of a discretely homosexual population distinct from the larger heterosexual population. Rather, by characterizing sexual orientation as a continuum, Kinsey challenged the widespread belief that, for most people, sexual desire is directed exclusively toward members of just one sex category. Moreover, by concentrating on homosexual behaviour instead of homosexual identity, Kinsey implicitly challenged what is sometimes referred to as *essentialism*. Essentialism is the belief that homosexuality and other identity categories reflect innate characteristics that comprise the fundamental nature of the members of those categories.[2] Because the essentialist account regards homosexuality as an enduring feature of the human condition, rather than the product of social contingencies, those who accept essentialism often assume that homosexuality is historically and culturally universal.

Social Construction

Some theorists who resist the popular assumption that the interests of lesbian women and gay men are best served by an essentialist perspective on homosexuality instead suggest that the categories associated with sexual pleasure and desire are historical and cultural developments. This thesis, often referred to as *social constructionism*,[3] applies to heterosexual identity as well as alternative sexual identity categories, such as homosexual, lesbian, gay, and bisexual. This does not mean that specific sexual acts are unique to the social contexts in which they occur. A wide range of physical interactions and bodily manipulations connected with sexual desire or conducive to sexual pleasure occur across cultural and historical boundaries. The relationship of these interactions and manipulations to socially entrenched concepts of sexuality and categories of sexual identity, however, is far from universal. As Jeffrey Weeks notes, 'the forces that shape and mould the erotic possibilities of the body vary from society to society' (Weeks, 2003).

This was the point of a landmark article, aptly titled 'The Homosexual Role' (1968), in which Mary McIntosh suggested that homosexuality is not a condition by which people are affected, but rather a social role to which people are assigned. According to McIntosh, 'the purpose of introducing the term "role" is to enable us to handle the fact that behavior in this sphere does not match popular beliefs: that sexual behavior patterns cannot be dichotomized in the way that the social roles of homosexual and heterosexual can' (1968, p.184). McIntosh addressed the influence of social role, specifically the role of homosexual male, on perceptions of both self and other:

In modern societies where a separate homosexual role is recognized, the expectation, on behalf of those who play the role and of others, is that a homosexual will be exclusively or very predominantly homosexual in his feelings and behavior. In addition, there are other expectations that frequently exist, especially on the part of nonhomosexuals, but affecting the self-conception of anyone who sees himself as homosexual. These are: the expectation that he will be effeminate in manner, personality, or preferred sexual activity; the expectation that sexuality will play a part of some kind in all his relations with other men; and the expectation that he will be attracted to boys and very young men and probably willing to seduce them.

(1968, pp.184–5)

Categories of identity determine and are determined by the ways in which people understand themselves and are understood by others. In other words, concepts of identity determine and are determined by the prescriptions and proscriptions that structure and are structured by social existence. Additionally, categories of identity are often *binary*, established by means of a contrast between the dominant group and those excluded from the dominant group.[4] Indeed, the term category ultimately derives from the ancient Greek word *kategoria*, meaning 'accusation' (Iannone, 2001, p.93).[5] In terms of sexual orientation, the dominant group is established by the distinction between normal and abnormal sexuality, coupled with the accusation that specific forms of sexuality are deviant. I am homosexual only in a culture that, first, has a definition of homosexuality and, second, has a definition of homosexuality that applies to me. Likewise, I am heterosexual only in a culture that, first, has a definition of homosexuality and, second, has a definition of homosexuality that applies to people other than me. The concept of heterosexuality, and hence heterosexual identity, could not exist without the concept of homosexuality, and hence homosexual identity. This inverts the customary way of thinking, in which heterosexuality is regarded as the primary, or original, form of sexuality and homosexuality is regarded as secondary, a mere variation on that first theme. For this reason, it has been suggested that, at least conceptually, homosexuality precedes heterosexuality (Katz, 1996). At the very least, homosexual and heterosexual identities emerge simultaneously and, more to the point, only in the context of a distinction between homosexuality and heterosexuality.[6]

The existence of both homosexuality and heterosexuality is contingent rather than necessary. To describe something as contingent is to claim that, under different circumstances, things could have turned out differently. This should not be confused with voluntarism regarding sexual identity. It is, as explained by Edward Stein, 'a mistake to collapse the distinction between social constructionism and essentialism into the distinction between determinism and voluntarism or *vice versa*' (1992, p.329). Social constructionism does not suggest that people are free to choose between homosexuality and heterosexuality. It does, however, suggest that the conceptual framework, or *paradigm*, within which homosexuality and heterosexuality occur is a historical development. To fully understand social constructionism, it is important to understand how paradigms function. For this reason, some background information about the concept of a paradigm may be useful.

Semantic Holism

The notion of a paradigm, as it is used here, is an extension of a concept introduced and developed in 1962 by Thomas Kuhn (1970) in reference to scientific practice. Kuhn maintained that the terminology employed within the various sciences is part of an interwoven web of beliefs, such that the meaning of any individual term is fully understood only by direct or indirect reference to the larger vocabulary and corresponding belief system. The indoctrination of scientists is largely a matter of language acquisition, and the language acquired determines standards of evidence and, hence, the range of empirical facts to be acknowledged and explained. This characterization is sometimes referred to as semantic *holism* and contrasted with semantic *atomism*. Whereas holism explains the individual parts by reference to the greater whole, atomism explains the whole by reference to its constituent parts.

This distinction is readily illustrated by ambiguous images conducive to two distinct and mutually exclusive visual interpretations. A familiar example is the black and white image alternately recognized as a vase against a dark background or a silhouette of two human faces (Figure 1.2).[7] Conceived as a vase, the image cannot be described by reference to terms such as forehead, nose, and chin; conceived as a pair of faces, the image cannot be described by reference to terms such as base, stem, and rim. The inference, for example, that the proximity of the lips is suggestive of a kiss makes sense only if the overall image is understood to represent a pair of faces. Indeed, the meaning of the term lip is quite different when applied to faces than when applied to vases. Kuhn maintained that the meaning of scientific terms is likewise dependent on the overall framework, or paradigm, in which those terms occur. Kuhn also maintained that, just as the ambiguous image is consistent with more than one interpretive framework, it is often the case that the empirical evidence is consistent with more than one paradigm.

This is not to be confused with wholesale *relativism*, which admits of no relationship between reality and interpretation, and no distinction between fact and fiction.[8] The claim that the ambiguous image can be meaningfully interpreted as a vase or as a pair of faces does not amount to the claim that the ambiguous image can be meaningfully interpreted as anything at all, however, nor does the claim that multiple paradigms are consistent with the empirical evidence amount to the claim that any possible paradigm would be consistent with the empirical evidence. What it does amount to is the claim that paradigms are sometimes *underdetermined* by the empirical evidence.[9] Because paradigms frame the interpretation of evidence, they often obscure the empirical adequacy of alternative paradigms. Viewers for whom the ambiguous image appears as two faces, if unable to switch paradigms, are overwhelmed by incontrovertible evidence that their interpretation is uniquely capable of accommodating the fact that the image consists of noses, lips, and various other facial features. Similarly, those 16th-century astronomers who were unable to make the switch from the geocentric paradigm to the heliocentric paradigm continued to define planetary movement as a change in position relative to earth and therefore dismissed the claim that the earth moved around the sun as utterly absurd.

Figure 1.2 Ambiguous vase-face image

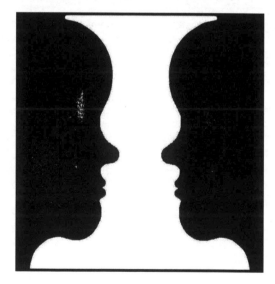

Cultural Variation

Although Kuhn introduced the notion of a paradigm within the specialized context of science, it can also be applied more broadly. Throughout history and across cultures, bodies have been known to mingle in various ways, but often without the requisite paradigm for the application of sexual identity categories specific to contemporary western culture. Consider, for example, the well-documented incidence of anal penetration between men in ancient Athens (Dover, 1978; Hubbard, 2003; Percy, 1996), which is often touted as evidence that homosexuality has existed throughout history (Dover, 1978; Hubbard, 2003). According to David Halperin, sex in ancient Athens 'served to position social actors in the places assigned to them, by virtue of their political standing, in the hierarchical structure of the Athenian polity' (Halperin, 1989 p.260). Adult male citizens occupied a higher social position than younger men, women, and slaves. Because 'sexual penetration was thematized as domination' (Halperin, 1989, p.260), it was consistent with the social role of the adult male citizen to seek sexual gratification not merely from women, but also from younger men and from slaves of any age or sex. Sexual relations between older and younger men is often referred to as *pederasty*.[10] As long as the dominant male took the dominant role, pederasty served to reinforce rather than threaten the social hierarchy. Within this hierarchy, however, the prospect of homosexuality, conceived as sexual partnership between social equals, would have seemed absurd. Where sex is defined as an act of domination through penetration, the notion of equal sexual partners is a contradiction in terms.

Although ancient Greek social structure sanctioned some acts of sexual penetration between men, it did not thereby condone, or even comprehend, anything quite like contemporary homosexuality. Similarly, the existence of various practices in non-western and Native American cultures is often touted as evidence that homosexuality exists across cultures (Nanda, 1990; Roscoe, 1991; Whitehead, 1981; Williams, 1986). As Harriet Whitehead notes:

> The homosexuality that other societies prescribe or condone is immediately taken to be something very much like one of the forms of homosexuality familiar to the modern West, and the explanation of the foreign culture's institutionalizing response, when offered, proceeds in accordance with the chosen meaning of the behavior in our own culture.
>
> (p.80)

The people identified in India as *hijras* provide one such example. The term *hijra* is applied to those born male or intersex[11] who undergo surgical castration in order to dress as women and inhabit an intermediate gender role. The people sometimes identified within Native American culture as *berdaches* provide another such example. Applied by anthropologists in reference to people who crossed gender lines in various Native American tribes, the term 'berdache' is regarded by some Native Americans as a careless, and sometimes offensive, alternative to the use of tribal names.[12] The Zuni, for example, used the term *lhamana* to refer to those who were born male and lived their adult lives as women (Roscoe, 1991). Similar people existed in many tribes and were believed to be two-spirited, simultaneously female and male. They often served as healers and performed sacred rituals. Though relevant to an analysis of social roles across cultures, such examples do not establish that homosexuality existed in Native America just as it exists in mainstream US culture today. After all, crossing gender lines in all aspects of social life is not a necessary feature, nor even a typical feature, of contemporary homosexual existence. For this reason, some may be tempted to equate this phenomenon in Native America not with homosexual identity, but rather with transgender identity.[13] This equivocation is mitigated by significant cultural differences: whereas Zuni *lhamanas* and similar people in other Native American tribes were revered as sacred, transgender identity in contemporary US culture is often met with sympathy, fear, ridicule, contempt, and even violence.

Beyond the Paradigm

Categories of sexual identity are unique to the cultural contexts through which they are defined. Contemporary western categories of sexual identity are usefully applied only to social contexts in which people define themselves and are defined by others in terms of their sexual desires and pleasures, when those definitions are analogous to the definitions supplied by contemporary western categories of sexual identity, and when those definitions generate experiences and expectations analogous to those associated with contemporary western categories of sexual identity. Phenomena such as pederasty in ancient Greece and gender-crossing in Native America suggest not that homosexuality is historically and culturally universal but rather that categories of sexual identity are historically and culturally specific. In other words, such examples suggest that categories of sexual identity are socially constructed.

Additional support for social construction is supplied by examples in which different cultures apply the nomenclature of sexual orientation differently. In mainstream US culture, for instance, men who engage in oral or anal sex with other men are generally labelled as gay – or perhaps bisexual, depending on whether they also engage sexually with women. According to Roger Lancaster (1987) and others (Almaguer, 1991; Carrier, 1976), however, this is not the case in Latin America where men who take the penetrative role in oral or anal sex with other men do not always identify as gay. While the receptive partner is stigmatized as passive, feminine, and therefore homosexual, there is no special category to describe the penetrative partner, who 'is not stigmatized at all' (Lancaster, 1987, p.113), despite a cultural stricture against homosexuality. A similar discontinuity between sexual behaviour and sexual identity has been documented in connection with some US Latino and Black subcultures (Hammonds, 1986; King, 2005).

Many regard such inconsistencies between sexual activity and sexual identity as *prima facie*[14] evidence of deceit. Given the social stigma against homosexual identity, it is not surprising that some people hide their homosexual desires from others and even, in some cases, from themselves. It is especially unfortunate that people occasionally achieve or maintain positions of power by publicly denouncing homosexuality despite their own privately homosexual existence. Such instances of blatant duplicity notwithstanding, there are also people whose sexuality is not adequately or accurately represented by either of the available identity categories – and the introduction of the intermediate third category of bisexuality does not always resolve the discrepancy. Consider ostensibly heterosexual women whose arousal is linked to fantasies about other women, or ostensibly heterosexual men whose arousal is linked to wearing feminine lingerie. Consider apparently heterosexual women who gain little pleasure from sexual relationships with men but submit to them for financial or social reasons, or apparently homosexual women who would gain much pleasure from sexual relationships with men but resist them for personal or political reasons. Also consider presumably heterosexual men who would gain equal pleasure from penetrating women, men, children, non-human animals, or inanimate objects, but for moral or legal reasons engage in sexual relationships with women only. Likewise consider allegedly bisexual women whose sexual relationships with other women give them only the indirect pleasure of serving the voyeuristic desires of their male partners. Consider those who admit that they had mutually satisfying sexual experiences with partners of the opposite sex before they 'came out' as lesbian or gay. Consider those with a distinct sexual preference for masculine women or feminine men, for transgender women or men, or for intersex partners. Finally, consider those for whom dominance or submission in the context of a bondage relationship is a more significant concern than the sex of a potential partner.

The identity categories bisexual, homosexual, and heterosexual neglect something significant about the sexuality of the people represented in these examples. For every case of wilful deception, there are perhaps far more in which people identify to themselves or to others as homosexual, bisexual, or heterosexual simply because more fitting categories are unavailable. The assumption that every perceived mismatch between sexual activity and sexual identity is an instance of deceit reflects and reinforces the essentialist thesis by taking for granted that the existing catalogue of identity categories provides an exhaustive and exclusive inventory of sexual possibilities. An alternative approach is to regard such mismatches as gaps in the established paradigm, and to use those gaps as points of entry in an examination of the social construction of that paradigm.

Additional Resources

- The Kinsey Institute. Selections from the 1947 and 1953 'Kinsey Reports' (http://www.kinseyinstitute.org/research/ak-data.html).
- McIntosh, M. (1968). 'The homosexual role'. *Social Problems*, 16(2), 182–92.
- Halperin, D. M. (1989). 'Is there a history of sexuality?'. *History and Theory* 28(3), 257–74.
- Nanda, S. (1990). 'Hijras as neither man nor woman'. *Neither Man Nor Woman: The Hijras of India*, pp.13–23. Belmont, CA: Wadsworth Publishing.
- Whitehead, H. (1981). 'The bow and the burden strap: A new look at institutionalized homosexuality in native North America'. In H. Whitehead and S. Ortner (eds), *Sexual Meanings: The Culture Construction of Gender and Sexuality*, pp.80–115. Cambridge: Cambridge University Press.
- Condon, B. (2004). *Kinsey*. Fox Searchlight Pictures.

References

Almaguer, T. (1991). 'Chicano men: A cartography of homosexual identity and behavior'. *differences: A Journal of Feminist Cultural Studies*, 3(2), 75–100.

Baum, L. F. (2005). *15 Books in 1: L. Frank Baum's Original 'Oz' Series*. Shoes and Ships and Sealing Wax, Ltd. (Original works published 1908–20).

Carrier, J. M. (1976). 'Cultural factors affecting urban Mexican male homosexual behavior'. *The Archives of Sexual Behavior*, 5(2), 103–24.

Condon, B. (2004). *Kinsey*. Fox Searchlight Pictures.

Dover, K. J. (1978). *Greek Homosexuality*. Cambridge: Harvard University Press.

Halperin, D. M. (1989). 'Is there a history of sexuality?'. *History and Theory* 28(3), 257–74.

Hammonds, E. (1986). 'Race, sex, AIDS: The construction of "other"'. *Radical American*, 20(6), 28–36.

Hubbard, T. K. (ed.) (2003). *Homosexuality in Ancient Greece and Rome: A Sourcebook of Basic Documents*. Berkeley: University of California Press.

Iannone, A. P. (2001). *Dictionary of World Philosophy*. London: Routledge.

Katz, J. N. (1996). *The Invention of Heterosexuality*. New York: Plume.

King, J. L. (2005). *On the Down Low: A Journey into the Lives of 'Straight' Black Men Who Sleep with Men*. New York: Harlem Moon.

Kinsey, A. C. (1941). 'Criteria for a hormonal explanation of the homosexual'. *Journal of Clinical Endocrinology and Metabolism*, 1, 424–8.

Kinsey, A. C., Pomeroy, W. B., and Martin, C. E. (1948). *Sexual Behavior in the Human Male*. Philadelphia: W. B. Saunders.

Kinsey, A. C., Pomeroy, W. B., Martin C. E., and Gebhard, P. H. (1953). *Sexual Behavior in the Human Female*. Philadelphia: W. B. Saunders.

The Kinsey Institute (n.d.). *Selected Research Findings from Kinsey's Studies*. Retrieved 22 March 2010 from http://www.kinseyinstitute.org/resources/bib-homoprev.html

The Kinsey Institute (June 1999). *Kinsey's Heterosexual-homosexual Rating Scale*. Retrieved 22 March 2010 from http://www.kinseyinstitute.org/research/ak-hhscale.html

Kuhn, T. S. (1970). *The Structure of Scientific Revolutions*. Chicago: University of Chicago Press (original work published in 1962).

Lancaster, R. N. (1987). 'Subject honor and object shame: The construction of male homosexuality and stigma in Nicaragua'. *Ethnology*, 27(2), 111–25.

Lang, S. (1998). *Men as Women, Women as Men: Changing Gender in Native American Cultures* (J. L. Vantine, trans.). Austin: University of Texas Press.

MacMullan, T. (2009). *Habits of Whiteness: A Pragmatist Reconstruction*. Bloomington: Indiana University Press.

McIntosh, M. (1968). 'The homosexual role'. *Social problems*, 16(2), 182–92.

Nanda, S. (1990). *Neither Man Nor Woman: The Hijras of India*. Belmont, CA: Wadsworth Publishing.

Percy, W. A., III. (1996). *Pederasty and Pedagogy in Archaic Greece*. Urbana: University of Illinois Press.

Roscoe, W. (1991). *The Zuni Man-woman*. Albuquerque: University of New Mexico Press.

Stein, E. (1992). *Forms of Desire: Sexual Orientation and the Social Constructionist Controversy*. New York: Routledge.

Weeks, J. (2003). *Sexuality* (2nd ed.). New York: Routledge (original work published in 1986).

Whitehead, H. (1981). 'The bow and the burden strap: A new look at institutionalized homosexuality in native North America'. In H. Whitehead and S. Ortner (eds), *Sexual Meanings: The Culture Construction of Gender and Sexuality*, pp.80–115. Cambridge: Cambridge University Press.

Williams, W. L. (1986). *The Spirit and the Flesh: Sexual Diversity in American Indian Culture*. Boston: Beacon Press.

Notes

1 In biology, the term bisexual refers to 'structures or individuals or aggregates of individuals that include the anatomy or functions of both sexes' (Kinsey, 1948 *et al.*, p.657). Because people inclined toward both homosexual and heterosexual expression are not marked by anatomical duality, however, Kinsey remarked that 'it is unfortunate to call such individuals bisexual' (1948, p.657).

2 Essentialism can be and has been applied to other identity categories as well, such as those connected with concepts of gender and race. In a more abstract sense, essentialism dates at least as far back as the ancient Greek philosopher Plato, who maintained that all general terms or categories reflect universal, eternal, pure, divine archetypes. Plato referred to these archetypes as *Forms* or *Ideas*, depending on the translation. This version of essentialism is usually contrasted with *nominalism*, according to which the only thing that unites the disparate members of any category is the contingent social fact that they happen to be given the same name. In response to Plato, for example, the ancient Greek philosopher Aristotle claimed that reality is comprised of individuals, or *tokens*, rather than universals, or *types*.

3 The decision to use the term social construct*ionism* rather than social construct*ivism* is primarily a matter of preference, which varies depending on the author. Social constructionism, like essentialism, can be and has been applied to other identity categories as well, such as those connected with concepts of gender and race. In a more general sense, social constructionism is the belief that reality, as it is known to human beings, is a product of human invention.

4 Binary refers to a dualism or dualistic division, usually in service of some form of essentialism.

5 Thanks to Ben Therrell for input regarding ancient Greek terminology.

6 A similar point can be made about other social categories including, for example, racial categories. As Terrance MacMullan notes, the 'history of whiteness shows how the boundaries of whiteness were defined primarily through the exclusion of those who were defined as non-white' (MacMullan, 2009, p.55).

7 As an alternative to this analogy, which may be inaccessible to readers with compromised vision, consider instead a tactile example. In an oft-cited parable, various individuals who lack the advantage of sight attempt to make sense of their experience when they encounter an elephant. Feeling the tail, one person employs the conceptual framework of a rope while, feeling the leg, another employs the conceptual framework of a tree, and so on. Without a conceptual framework that takes the whole elephant into account, they are unable to fully understand the individual components. To understand the tail as a tail, rather than a rope, requires a shift in paradigm.

8 It is also useful to differentiate between descriptive and prescriptive forms of relativism. While descriptive relativism amounts to the fairly uncontroversial notion that beliefs and practices vary from person to person and from culture to culture, prescriptive relativism therefore concludes that no meaningful distinction can be made between better and worse beliefs and practices. Not every reference to relativism goes to the extreme of eliminating the distinction between fact and fiction, but there is a prevalent concern that challenging notions of absolute truth and objective reality begins the descent down a slippery slope in that direction.

9 Although it is not necessarily the case that *every* theory and *every* paradigm is consistent with the empirical evidence, it is often the case that multiple theories and multiple paradigms are consistent with the empirical evidence. For this reason, evidence alone is often insufficient to determine the choice of one theory or one paradigm over another. To put it another way, theories and paradigms are often underdetermined. Underdetermination is a difficult but important concept, and it is addressed in more detail in Chapter 3.

10 While pederasty refers, literally, to the love of boys, it is generally used to identify sexual relations between an adult male and a male who is younger, but past the age of puberty. Pederasty is distinguished from pedophilia, which refers to sexual relations between any adult and a prepubescent boy or girl.

11 Intersex refers to people who were born with biological characteristics that do not differentiate them as clearly biologically female, nor as clearly biologically male. In many cases, intersex people are subject to medical intervention shortly after birth to facilitate a closer match between their physical presentation and a recognizably feminine or masculine gender identity. Historically, the term hermaphrodite was used to refer to certain forms of what is now more commonly

identified as intersex. The term hermaphrodite is potentially misleading if used to refer generically to all intersex bodies. It implies the presence of both male and female genitals, but not all intersex bodies match this characterization. Although some people prefer to be identified as hermaphrodites, more people prefer the designation of intersex. Moreover, some regard hermaphrodite as outdated, insensitive, and even offensive. Intersex is discussed in more detail in Chapter 4.

12 For a discussion of gender-crossing and the terminology used to describe it in various Native American cultures, refer to Sabine Lang, *Men as Women, Women as Men* (1998).

13 Transgender refers to people were born as biological females but identify internally, and often socially, as men, as well as people who were born as biological males but identify internally, and often socially, as women. Some, but certainly not all, transgender men and women seek medical intervention to facilitate a closer match between their physical presentation and the identity they experience internally. Transgender identity is discussed in more detail in Chapter 5.

14 *Prima facie* is a Latin expression that literally means 'on first appearance'.

2

The Social History of Lesbian and Gay Identity

*There are wild beasts in the woods, and a race of queer men who
do not like strangers to cross their country.*
(L. Frank Baum, *The Wonderful Wizard of Oz*, p.34)

Social Histories of Homosexual Identity

An early theory about the social construction of homosexuality,
introduced in Mary McIntosh's 1968 article 'The Homosexual Role' and
developed in Alan Bray's book *Homosexuality in Renaissance England*,
first published in 1982, is that homosexual identity, particularly among
men, emerged with the proliferation of establishments, particularly
taverns, conducive to casual social contact.[1] McIntosh noted that 'a
rudimentary homosexual subculture' (1968, p.187) began to develop
in England toward the end of the 17th century as men with a shared
interest in sexual interaction with other men came together in taverns
and private dwellings. These men came to be known as 'mollies' and
their gathering places as 'molly houses'. 'The molly houses', according
to Bray, 'were scattered across the whole of the built up area north of
the Thames' (1995, p.84) and they 'merged into a coherent social milieu'
(1995, p.85). Mollies and molly houses eventually attracted the attention
of the Societies for the Reformation of Manners, a religious organization
that existed to 'lay information before the magistrates against sabbath-
breakers, drunkenness and debauchery' (Bray, 1995, p.89). In 1726, this
attention led to a series of raids, arrests, and trials, and it culminated in
the execution of those found guilty of sodomy or buggery.[2]

Although religious condemnation of sodomy was not new, according
to Bray, the distinct subculture associated with the molly houses provided
a specifiable target for existing hostilities:

There was now a continuing culture to be fixed on and an extension of the area in which homosexuality could be expressed and therefore recognised; clothes, gestures, language, particular buildings and particular public places – all could be identified as having specifically homosexual connotations. In contrast, the socially diffused homosexuality of the earlier seventeenth century was far less obtrusive.... Its successor in the world of molly houses was something that could easily be seen, and it was this that brought upon it the persecution which for so long had been often no more than an unrealised potential. Its visibility was its bane.

(Bray, 1995, p.92)

Prior to the emergence of this new subculture, sodomy was thought of as a 'disorder in sexual relations that, in principle, at least, could break out anywhere' (Bray, 1995, p.25). The transfer of negative attitudes associated with sodomy onto this subculture marked the evolution of homosexuality as a social role.

McIntosh's 'The Homosexual Role' was among the earliest published accounts of the social construction of homosexual identity, but it took almost a decade and the publication of Michel Foucault's *The History of Sexuality, Volume 1* (released in French in 1976 and first translated into English in 1977) for the thesis to gain momentum. Unlike McIntosh, who regarded homosexuality as an 18th-century innovation, Foucault supplied a later date and a different causal mechanism. According to Foucault, homosexual identity emerged in connection with the scientific research of the late 19th century.[3] Informed by both McIntosh and Foucault, Bray pursued McIntosh's suggestion that homosexuality emerged in connection with the molly houses of the early 18th century, and thereby provided an alternative to Foucault's increasingly popular account of the origin of homosexual identity.

Foucault's analysis of the *discourses* surrounding sexuality during the Victorian era[4] and into the 20th century (Foucault, 1990) is widely celebrated as the first detailed articulation of the social construction of homosexuality. Foucault used the term discourse, not simply in reference to dialogue or discussion, but instead to refer more broadly to 'ways of constituting knowledge, together with the social practices, forms of subjectivity and power relations which inhere in such knowledges and relations between them' (Weedon, 1987, p.108). Although the Victorians are usually portrayed as sexually repressed, Foucault noted that a variety of discourses about sexuality began to emerge and multiply during the 19th century. Describing this period in terms of its growing preoccupation with sexuality, Foucault challenged the commonly accepted 'repressive hypothesis', which alleges that a gradual repression of sexuality began in the 17th century, reached its peak during the Victorian period, and is finally beginning to give way to more reasonable attitudes.

Foucault asked a series questions to cast doubt on the repressive hypothesis. First, 'Is sexual repression truly an established historical fact? Is what first comes into view – and consequently permits one to advance an initial hypothesis – really the accentuation or even the establishment of a regime of sexual repression beginning in the seventeenth century?' In addition, 'Do the workings of power, and in particular those mechanisms that are brought into play in societies such as ours, really belong primarily to the category of repression? Are prohibition, censorship, and denial truly the forms through which power is exercised in a general way, if not in every society, most certainly in our own?' And finally, 'Did the critical discourse that addresses itself to repression come to act as a roadblock to a power mechanism that had operated unchallenged up to that point, or is it not in fact part of the same historical network as the thing it denounces (and doubtlessly misrepresents) by calling it "repression"? Was there really a historical rupture between the age of repression and the critical analysis of repression?' (1990, p.10)

The repressive hypothesis ignores what Foucault (1990), borrowing an expression from Steven Marcus (1966), referred to as the 'other Victorians'. Not only prostitutes, pimps, and their clients, but also psychiatrists and their patients, as well as many others with an unmistakable interest in sexuality, serve as counter-examples to the alleged ubiquity of repression among Victorians. As Foucault was quick to explain, however, the relevant issue is not so much to determine whether sexuality is affirmed or denied, encouraged or discouraged, but rather 'to account for the fact that it is spoken about, to discover who does the speaking, the positions and viewpoints from which they speak, the institutions which prompt people to speak about it and which store and distribute the things that are said' (1990, p.11). As it turns out, much of the 19th-century discourse surrounding sexuality was created and controlled by various scientific and pseudo-scientific disciplines concerned with delineating the boundaries between acceptable (normal, natural) and unacceptable (peripheral, perverse) forms of sexuality.

> Through the various discourses, legal sanctions against minor perversions were multiplied; sexual irregularity was annexed to mental illness; from childhood to old age, a norm of sexual development was defined and all possible deviations were carefully described; pedagogical controls and medical treatments were organized; around the least fantasies, moralists, but especially doctors, brandished the whole emphatic vocabulary of abomination.
>
> (Foucault, 1990, p.36)

The 'persecution of the peripheral sexualities' (Foucault, 1990, p.42) established 'a new *specification of individuals*' (1990, pp.42–3).

This new specification of individuals meant that people came to be defined in terms of their sexual desires and pleasures. Prior to this development, various forms of sexual expression, particularly sodomy, were prohibited by law and religion, but were regarded as ordinary temptations, like promiscuity or adultery, against which anyone might struggle, but they did not constitute categories of personal or social identity. With the new specification of individuals, the pervert – rather, a vast range of perverts – came into existence.[5]

The nineteenth-century homosexual became a personage, a past, a case history, and a childhood, in addition to being a type of life, a life form, and a morphology, with an indiscreet anatomy and possibly a mysterious physiology. Nothing that went into his total composition was unaffected by his sexuality. It was everywhere present in him: at the root of all his actions because it was their insidious and indefinitely active principle; written immodestly on his face and body because it was a secret that always gave itself away. It was consubstantial with him, less as a habitual sin than as a singular nature.

(Foucault, 1990, p.43)

For Foucault, then, contemporary western conceptions of homosexuality emerged with the formulation and proliferation of discourses on sexuality, particularly medical discourses, during a period associated, ironically, with the suppression of sexuality.

Following Foucault, John D'Emilio (1983) rejected the 'myth of the "eternal homosexual"' (p.101) and associated the advent of homosexual identity with the late 19th century. Unlike Foucault, however, D'Emilio attributed this development to the emergence of capitalism and wage labour, through which people gained independence from the more traditional extended family household.

I want to argue that gay men and lesbians have *not* always existed. Instead, they are a product of history, and have come into existence in a specific historical era. Their emergence is associated with the relations of capitalism; it has been the historical development of capitalism – more specifically, its free labor system – that has allowed large numbers of men and women in the late twentieth century to call themselves gay, to see themselves as part of a community of similar men and women, and to organize politically on the basis of that identity.

(D'Emilio, 1983, p.102)

With capitalism came a gradual shift away from the family farm as the unit of production. As more people, especially men, became engaged in wage work outside the home, 'the family took on new significance as an affective unit, an institution that produced not goods but emotional satisfaction and happiness' (D'Emilio, 1983, p.103). No longer a matter of economic necessity, the family became a retreat from the 'public world of work and production' (D'Emilio, 1983, p.103).

In addition, the significance of procreation waned because the labour of children was no longer necessary. According to D'Emilio, this led to changing attitudes about the role of sexual relations within marriage.

The meaning of heterosexual relations also changed. In colonial New England, the birthrate averaged over seven children per woman of childbearing age. Men and women needed the labor of children. Producing offspring was as necessary for survival as producing grain. Sex was harnessed to procreation. The puritans did not celebrate *hetero*sexuality but rather marriage; they condemned *all* sexual expression outside the marriage bond and did not differentiate sharply between sodomy and heterosexual fornication.

(D'Emilio, 1983, p.104)

Sexual relations, which no longer served an essential economic function, joined the family unit as a source of intimacy in a private space clearly delineated from the public world. There is evidence that various forms of sexual expression associated with homosexuality occurred in earlier times (D'Emilio, 1983, p.104), but only when individuals came to represent isolated economic agents did it become possible 'to remain outside the heterosexual family and to construct a personal life based on attraction to one's own sex' (D'Emilio, 1983, p.105).

Like McIntosh, Bray, and Foucault, D'Emilio drew a distinction between sexual activity and sexual identity. Again like McIntosh, Bray, and Foucault, D'Emilio noted that, although homosexual activity was not condoned prior to the evolution of a specifically homosexual identity, it also was not condemned more harshly than other transgressions, such as promiscuity and adultery. In Bray's words, 'temptation to debauchery, from which homosexuality was not distinguished, was accepted as part of the common lot' (Bray, 1995, p.16). To put it another way, homosexuality was regarded, not as a form of deviance, but as a form of indulgence. Regardless of its origins, the emergence of homosexuality as an identity category resulted in a contrast between heterosexual desire as normal or natural and homosexual desire as abnormal or unnatural.

The specification of seemingly different causal factors by McIntosh and Bray, Foucault, and D'Emilio does not render their analyses incompatible. The time frame for the inception of homosexual identity supplied by D'Emilio coincides with the time frame supplied by Foucault, though D'Emilio attributed causality to changing social structures and Foucault attributed it to the emerging medical discourses. It is unlikely, however, that 19th-century medical discourses were completely uninformed by concurrent social changes. Indeed, the industrial revolution, which was the background for the transition from family farming to wage labour, was characterized by a sense of optimism regarding the use of science and technology to improve the human condition. Thus, the proliferation of medical discourses simultaneous with industrialization and the wage labour system was hardly a matter of mere coincidence. According to McIntosh and Bray, homosexual identity emerged much earlier, but only in a developed part of London during a period of urban growth. If the urban lifestyle associated with industrialization contributed to the development of homosexual identity, then it makes sense that it would have appeared in this particular region before reaching other parts of England or the USA. While neither Bray nor D'Emilio explain the emergence of homosexual identity among poor men or men in rural areas, they do offer a plausible explanation of the emergence of a collective gay identity for at least some men at the time.

Social Histories of Lesbian Identity

Homosexuality is not, in principle, a gendered concept. Theoretically, it refers equally to female homosexuality and male homosexuality. Nevertheless, the social histories supplied by McIntosh, Bray, and Foucault are concentrated almost exclusively on male homosexual identity. D'Emilio's (1983) discussion is the exception, reserving the generic term, homosexual, for reference to both women and men, and substituting the gendered terms, lesbian and gay,[6] to differentiate between the two. In addition, D'Emilio dealt directly, albeit briefly, with the evolution of lesbian identity. According to D'Emilio, the evolution of lesbian identity, like the evolution of gay male identity, became possible only with economic independence from the traditional family structure. Despite the shift to the wage labour system, however, many women remained financially dependent on men well into the 20th century. Still relegated to the private world of home and family, women lacked access to the social world of taverns and public houses in which the parameters of the male homosexual role seem to have been negotiated.

It is therefore not surprising that, until fairly recently, female homosexuality did not attract as much attention as male homosexuality. According to Annamarie Jagose, 'female homosexuality does not occupy the same positions as male homosexuality in the discourses of law or medicine' (Jagose, 1996, p.13). When male homosexuality was publicly condemned, the possibility of female homosexuality was often ignored:

For example, the internationally influential British judicial system – which during Britain's colonial period was adopted or enforced as the legal template in many other countries – criminalised male homosexual acts while ignoring the possibility of female homosexuality. The Labouchère Amendment of 1885, on which much current anti-homosexual western legislation is founded, specifically outlaws acts of 'gross indecency' between 'male persons,' but leaves comparable acts between female persons legal by default. Similarly – and partly as a consequence of its different relation to criminalisation – female homosexuality took much longer than male homosexuality to constitute the basis of a communal, subcultural identity.

(Jagose, 1996, p.13)

The medical community did not acknowledge female homosexuality until late 19th- and early 20th-century sexologists addressed what they referred to as 'sexual inversion', a condition believed to be characterized by the complete reversal of gender, including sexual attraction toward members of the same sex. In particular, Richard von Krafft-Ebing's *Psychopathia Sexualis* was published in German in 1886 and in English in 1892 (Krafft-Ebing, 2007), and Havelock Ellis' *Sexual Inversion* was published in 1897 (Ellis, 2007). The ideas of Krafft-Ebing and Ellis were then popularized in Radclyffe Hall's 1928 novel *The Well of Loneliness* (Hall, 1990), for which Ellis wrote the foreword. The confusion felt by the novel's protagonist, Stephen, a masculine woman who experiences sexual love for other women, reflects the absence, outside of the medical community, of a clearly defined female homosexual social role. The decision to ban the book in both the UK and the USA suggests that at least some people were reluctant to entertain the concept of female homosexuality, while the publication in England of three additional lesbian-themed novels[7] in 1928 suggests that others had already begun to extend the distinction between homosexuality and heterosexuality to female sexuality.

Under the old paradigm, there was no concept of female homosexuality. As described by Vicinus, however, there were at least four distinct characterizations of 18th-century European and North American women who deviated from traditional feminine roles. First, there was the 'passing woman' who dressed as a man and, often enough, was sufficiently convincing to obtain work, freedom, or the opportunity to serve in the military.

Eighteenth-century broadside ballads praised the 'female warrior' who went into battle in order to find her beloved. Most versions raised the possibility of sexual transgression but resolved matters in the final verse with a happy marriage or other appropriate female destiny.

(Vicinus, 1992, pp.473–4)

This behaviour was readily cast as heterosexual and hence unproblematic. Second, and more problematic, however, was the 'mannish woman'. Included in this category were women who continued dressing as men even after the end of the war. Third, there was the sexually 'free woman'. 'Her appearance and behavior could signal an erotic interest in women, but at other times – as prostitute, courtesan, or mistress – she chose men' (Vicinus, 1992, p.475). Finally, there were women engaged in 'romantic friendship', as outlined by Lillian Faderman in *Surpassing the Love of Men* (1981). According to Vicinus, these four characterizations 'were united less by the behavior or attitudes of the women than by the ways in which men interpreted women's same-sex desire' (1992, p.477).

Lillian Faderman (1981) noted that, prior to the 20th century, female romantic friendships, which may or may not have involved sexual intimacy, were not merely ignored, but were actually encouraged. Faderman suggested that public recognition of the possibility of sexual intimacy within female romantic friendships, and corresponding condemnation of such friendships, occurred only in response to the demand for social change issued by the first wave of feminism.[8] This is consistent with Martha Vicinus' (1992) claim that condemnation of female homosexuality, when it occurs, is a direct result of male insecurities. 'Only when a woman seemed to contravene directly masculine priorities and privileges was she punished' (Vicinus, 1992, p.477).

For both Faderman and Vicinus, public recognition and condemnation of lesbian identity represented a hostile reaction, or *backlash*, against actual or perceived threats to male authority and privilege. For D'Emilio, the formation of lesbian identity, like the formation of gay male identity, became possible as the result of increased independence from the traditional family structure. The independence of women from the traditional family structure was not an immediate or inevitable consequence of the shift from family farming to a wage economy, however, and if women of the early 20th century enjoyed sufficient freedom to entertain lesbian alternatives to traditional marriage, this was certainly attributable, at least in part, to progress made by the women's movement.

The first convention on women's rights was held in Seneca Falls, New York, in 1848, organized by some of the same women[9] who fought, successfully, for the passage of the New York Married Women's Property Act that same year. The Married Women's Property Act allowed women to retain control over their own property after marriage, thus granting at least some women greater economic independence from men while simultaneously threatening the authority and privilege of at least some men. The National Woman Suffrage Association was formed in 1869, followed by the American Woman Suffrage Association. The two groups merged in 1890, forming the National American Woman Suffrage Association, and had established a national headquarters in New York by 1900. Although it took another twenty years and the successful passage of the 19th amendment to gain voting rights for women in 1920, the feminist threat to the system of male authority and privilege was clearly well established by the turn of the century.[10]

Given this connection between women's independence and the threat to male authority and privilege, the accounts offered by D'Emilio, Faderman, and Vicinus are actually compatible regarding the emergence of lesbian identity. Unlike D'Emilio, however, Faderman and Vicinus drew attention to the role of what Suzanne Pharr (1988) referred to as *lesbian-baiting*. Lesbian-baiting occurs when women are labelled as lesbians, not for engaging sexually with other women, but for other perceived violations of assigned gender roles. In particular, women who embody feminist principles are often characterized as lesbians. By equating feminist identity with lesbian identity, lesbian-baiting is an attempt, often successful, to capitalize on negative attitudes about homosexuality to prevent women from identifying as feminists.

Even if public recognition and condemnation of lesbian identity was largely a matter of lesbian-baiting and backlash, there was a growing population of women who enjoyed the requisite independence to gather with other women and, in some cases, forge lesbian identities that would have been impossible in earlier generations. Despite the existence of women who now identified and were identified by others as homosexual, they seem to have been more isolated and dispersed than the men who participated in the formation of a cohesive and recognizable gay male subculture. This lack of cohesion among lesbian women is reflected in the fact that, Faderman's discussion of female romantic friendships aside, little attempt has been made to offer a single account of the social construction of female homosexual identity. Instead, a number of ethnographic studies have addressed the evolution of lesbian identity in specific, local contexts. In *Boots of Leather, Slippers of Gold*, for example, Elizabeth Kennedy and Madeline Davis (1993) detail the experiences of women who were part of the working-class lesbian subculture in Buffalo, New York, during the 1940s and 50s. Similarly, in *Cherry Grove, Fire Island*, Esther Newton (1993) offers an account of life in what was perhaps the first lesbian and gay resort community in the USA. In addition to ethnographic studies, there are many autobiographical accounts tracing the evolution of lesbian identity in the lives of particular women.

Isolated expressions of lesbian identity were not unified by a cohesive and recognizable subculture, and emerging cultural ideas about lesbian identity were not unified by a single set of expectations. As expressed by Vicinus: 'Lesbian desire is everywhere, even as it may be nowhere. Put bluntly, we lack any general agreement about what constitutes a lesbian' (1992, p.468). Even today, there seems to be little consensus regarding lesbian identity. Consider, for example, that in some contexts, particularly mainstream pornography,[11] lesbian sexuality is often portrayed as integral to heterosexual male fantasy, while in other contexts, particularly the backlash against feminism, both feminists and lesbians are characterized as sexually unappealing to heterosexual men. With respect to gay male identity, a single stereotype dominates mainstream culture, and this stereotype has changed very little, if at all, since the 17th-century characterization of homosexual men as mollies. While many gay men seek to distance themselves from this stereotype, both lesbian women and feminist women who attempt to distance themselves from one of the stereotypes – for example, of lesbian women as objects of heterosexual male fantasy – inevitably find themselves situated that much closer to another stereotype – for example, of feminist women as the antithesis to heterosexual male desire. This is a concern for lesbian women, regardless of whether they identify as feminists, and for feminist women, regardless of whether they identify as lesbians.

The point of this observation is not to suggest that the expectations associated with lesbian identity are any more or less restrictive than those associated with gay male identity, but simply to note that they are less consistent and less cohesive than the expectations associated with gay male identity. Precisely because they are neither consistent nor cohesive, however, they demonstrate that there is room within contemporary western culture to accommodate multiple interpretations of lesbian identity and, presumably, of other sexual identities as well. This serves as an invitation to introduce alternative interpretations of sexual identities that lie outside the heterosexual norm, particularly interpretations that will better serve the interests of those who do not conform to the heterosexual norm. In other words, it serves as an invitation to construct an alternative paradigm of sexuality. More specifically, it is an invitation to construct a paradigm in which those who identify as lesbian, gay, bisexual, and heterosexual – regardless of whether they are transgender men and women, biological women and men, or intersex persons – along with those who define their sexuality in different terms or not all, may at the same time exhibit characteristics and express themselves in ways that might be deemed feminine, masculine, both, or neither.

Additional Resources

- Foucault, M. (1990). 'Part three: Scientia sexualis', *The History of Sexuality, Volume 1: An Introduction* (R. Hurley, trans.), pp.51–73. New York: Vintage Books.
- D'Emilio, J. (1983). 'Capitalism and gay identity'. In A. Snitow, C. Stansell, and S. Thompson (eds), *Powers of Desire: The Politics of Sexuality* (pp.100–13). New York: Monthly Review Press.
- Newton, E. (1993). 'Just one of the boys', *Cherry Grove, Fire Island: Sixty Years in America's First Gay and Lesbian Town*, pp.221–34. Boston: Beacon Press.
- Vicinus, M. (1992). '"They wonder to which sex I belong": The historical

roots of the modern lesbian identity'. *Feminist Studies* 28(3), 467–97.
• Finch, N. (1996). *Stonewall*. BBC Warner.

References

Baum, L. F. (2005). *15 Books in 1: L. Frank Baum's Original 'Oz' Series*. Shoes and Ships and Sealing Wax, Ltd. (original works published 1908–20).

Bray, A. (1995). *Homosexuality in Renaissance England* (2nd ed.). New York: Columbia University Press.

D'Emilio, J. (1983). Capitalism and gay identity. In A. Snitow, C. Stansell, and S. Thompson (eds), *Powers of Desire: The Politics of Sexuality* (pp.100–13). New York: Monthly Review Press.

Ellis, H. (2007). *Studies in the Psychology of Sex, Volume 2: Sexual Inversion*. Charleston, SC: BiblioBazaar, LLC (original work published in 1897).

Faderman, L. (1981). *Surpassing the Love of Men: Romantic Friendship and Love between Women from the Renaissance to the Present*. New York: William Morrow & Co.

Finch, N. (1996). *Stonewall*. BBC Warner.

Foucault, M. (1990). *The History of Sexuality, Volume 1: An Introduction* (R. Hurley, trans.). New York: Vintage Books (original work published in French in 1976).

Hall, R. (1990). *The Well of Loneliness: A 1920s Classic of Lesbian Fiction*. New York: Anchor Books (original work published in 1928).

Jagose, A. (1996). *Queer Theory: An Introduction*. New York: NYU Press.

Kennedy, E. and Davis, M. (1993). *Boots of Leather, Slippers of Gold: The History of a Lesbian Community*. New York: Routledge.

Krafft-Ebing, R. V. (2007). *Psychopathia Sexualis: With Especial Reference to the Antipathic Sexual Instinct, a Medico-forensic Study* (F. J. Rebman, trans.). Whitefish, MT: Kessinger Publishing, LLC (original work published in 1892).

Marcus, S. (1966). *The Other Victorians*. New York: Basic Books.

McIntosh, M. (1968). 'The homosexual role'. *Social Problems*, 16(2), 182–92.

Money, J. (1988). *Gay, Straight, and In-between: The Sexology of Erotic Orientation*. New York: Oxford University Press.

Newton, E. (1993). *Cherry Grove, Fire Island: Sixty Years in America's First Gay and Lesbian Town*. Boston: Beacon Press.

Pharr, S. (1988). *Homophobia: A Weapon of Sexism*. Berkeley: Chardon Press.

Schneir, M. (ed.) (1994). *Feminism: The Essential Historical Writings*. New York: Vintage Books.

Vicinus, M. (1992). '"They wonder to which sex I belong": The historical roots of the modern lesbian identity'. *Feminist Studies* 28(3), 467–97.

Weedon, C. (1987). *Feminist Practice and Poststructuralist Theory*. Oxford: Blackwell.

Notes

1 The decision, in this chapter, to present the histories of homosexual and gay men before presenting the history of lesbian identity has the disadvantage of

participating in the familiar habit of symbolically positioning men ahead of women. It nevertheless offers the benefit of mimicking the order in which these identity categories entered the collective consciousness of western culture. While gay identity was hidden throughout much of history, lesbian identity remained hidden for even longer, and this is reflected in the way the material unfolds throughout this chapter.

2 Today, sodomy is often used to refer specifically to anal sex, but it also refers more generally to any sexual intercourse other than when penis is received by vagina. Buggery, used primarily in England, has similar connotations.

3 More specifically, Foucault cited the 1870 publication of an article by Westphal as the date homosexuality first emerged (Foucault, 1990, p.43).

4 The Victorian era is associated with the reign of Queen Victoria from 1837 to 1901 during what many regard as the height of the British Empire. The transition from agriculture to industry during this period had tremendous impact on political interests, economic relations, class structure, and many other aspects of social life.

5 In keeping with the 19th-century trend of proliferating perversions, the contemporary sexologist John Money has generated a list of more than fifty specific *paraphilias* (1988, pp.179–80). Although the use of the term paraphilia avoids making outdated reference to perversion, it nevertheless refers to 'unusual and personally or socially unacceptable' forms of sexual pleasure and desire (Money, 1988, p.216).

6 Gay is sometimes used, like homosexual, to refer to homosexuality among women as well as men. More often, however, gay is used in reference to homosexuality among men, whereas lesbian is used in reference to homosexuality among women.

7 Following the publication of Radclyffe Hall's *The Well of Loneliness*, Elizabeth Bowen's *The Hotel*, Virginia Woolf's *Orlando*, and Compton MacKenzie's *Extraordinary Women*, all of which contained lesbian themes, were also published in England in 1928.

8 A distinction is often drawn between the first, second, and third waves of feminism. The first wave refers to the women's movement of the 19th and early 20th centuries, which gained its greatest momentum in connection with women's suffrage, or voting rights, in the USA. Enthusiasm waned following the ratification of the 19th amendment in 1920, but momentum returned in the early 1960s in connection with growing concern over the persistence of women's social and economic oppression. There is disagreement about whether feminism has entered yet a third wave. While some regard contemporary feminism as a continuation of the second wave, others regard the recent attention to differences among women's definitions of self as an emerging hallmark of the third wave and a break from the legal and economic concerns of an earlier generation. Third-wave feminism is discussed in more detail in Chapter 7 and Chapter 8.

9 Examples include Lucretia Mott, Ernestine Rose, and Elizabeth Cady Stanton.

10 For a more thorough examination of the first wave of the women's movement, refer to the edited collection *Feminism: The Essential Historical Writings* (Schneir, 1994).

11 The reference to mainstream pornography, rather than a reference simply to pornography, recognizes that attempts have been made to produce pornography from a feminist perspective and without the usual sexist trappings.

3

Queer Alternatives

The Wizard did not know how powerful the queer beast might be, so he resolved to take no chances.
(L. Frank Baum, *The Magic of Oz*, p.557)

Paradigm Change

Kuhn's (1970) discussion of the role of paradigms within science includes an account of paradigm change, or the transition from one conceptual framework to another. Recognizing that sexuality, like science, is a human *practice*, a useful analogy can be drawn between paradigm change in the context of science and paradigm change in the context of sexuality. The term practice is used here not in reference to repetition or rehearsal, but rather to patterns of social behaviour and interaction. Karl Marx, for example, described practice as 'sensuous human activity' (1970, p.121) and remarked that 'coincidence of the changing of circumstances and of human activity or self-changing can be conceived and rationally understood only as *revolutionary practice*' (1970, p.121). Just as Marx made reference to revolutionary practice, Kuhn made reference to revolutionary science. For Kuhn, normal scientific practice, characterized by consensus around an established paradigm, is contrasted with revolutionary scientific practice, characterized by crisis and conflict.

A parallel exists between paradigm change, or revolution, in the context of scientific practice and paradigm change, or revolution, in the larger context of political practice:

Political revolutions are inaugurated by a growing sense, often restricted to a segment of the political community, that existing institutions have ceased adequately to meet the problems posed by an environment that they have in part created. In much the same way, scientific revolutions are inaugurated by a growing sense, again often restricted to a narrow subdivision of the scientific community, that an existing paradigm has ceased to function adequately in the exploration of an aspect of nature to which that paradigm itself had previously led the way.

(1970, p.92)

In scientific practice and in political practice, crisis, along with a corresponding potential for revolution, occurs when the established paradigm ceases to accommodate the world it helped to create. Similarly, the established paradigm of sexuality, which initially provided a tidy distinction between homosexuality as deviant and heterosexuality as normal, has ceased to accommodate the various and often subtle ways in which sexuality deviates from the heterosexual norm. This is especially clear in connection with transgender identity. Consider, for example, the tendency to classify Hall's *The Well of Loneliness* as a 'lesbian novel', though its protagonist exhibits an identity that could just as readily be characterized as transgender. The conflation of transgender and homosexual identities is consistent with the late 19th- and early 20th-century account of 'sexual inversion', but it is inconsistent with the existence of lesbian women and gay men who are otherwise typical in terms of gender expression. It is also inconsistent with the existence of transgender men and women whose sexuality is oriented toward members of the same gender category to which they have transitioned.

In the context of science, Kuhn noted, there 'are always difficulties in the paradigm-nature fit', but these are usually resolved in the course of normal scientific practice (1970, p.82). The fit between paradigm and nature, or between theories and facts, is never perfect, and much of normal scientific practice, and perhaps much of normal practice in other contexts, consists of what Kuhn referred to as the 'mop-up work' (1970, p.24) of extending and articulating the accepted paradigm. Not all messes are easily mopped up, however, and not all mismatches between paradigm and nature are easily reconciled. When an especially stubborn mismatch between paradigm and nature 'comes to seem more than just another puzzle of normal science', according to Kuhn, 'the transition to crisis and to extraordinary science has begun' (1970, p.82). Kuhn maintained that 'all crises begin with the blurring of a paradigm and the consequent loosening of the rules for normal research' (p.84). Perhaps at least some perceived mismatches between sexual identity and sexual behaviour represent especially stubborn mismatches between paradigm and nature. Perhaps they represent a blurring of the paradigm of sexuality and a consequent loosening of the rules for applying the categories of sexual identity. Perhaps, then, contemporary western culture has entered a period of crisis in connection with the paradigm by which sexual practice is characterized.

Kuhn claimed that, within scientific practice, closure to such crises inevitably follows one of three paths. First, the problem that provoked the crisis may be resolved in the course of normal science, often through subtle refinements to the paradigm. Second, the unresolved problem may be set aside with the expectation that eventually it will submit to the efforts of normal science. Finally, an alternative paradigm may emerge, along with 'the ensuing battle over its acceptance' (Kuhn, 1970, p.84). In the first case, the problem is resolved by making adjustments to the existing paradigm. In the third case, the problem is resolved by replacing the existing paradigm. If resolution is finally achieved in the second case, in which the problem is merely postponed, it would seem to constitute an extension of the first case; if resolution is not achieved before the paradigm is replaced, it would seem to constitute an extension of the third case. Ultimately, then, crisis resolution demands either a change within the existing paradigm or a more revolutionary transition to an alternative paradigm.

Indeed, the accepted paradigm of sexuality has undergone a series of adjustments in an effort to account for the existence of a wide range of people who do not conform to the heterosexual norm. Consider the expanded and expanding inventory of identities collectively addressed in connection with the effort to secure freedom of sexual expression.[1] An early example of such effort is found in the homophile movement of the late 19th and early 20th centuries. Homosexual men began to form homophile organizations in Europe 'in the same period in which homosexuality crystallised as an identity, when for the first time it was possible to *be* a homosexual' (Jagose, 1996, p.22). These organizations upheld the rights of homosexuals by noting the consensus within the medical community around the notion of homosexuality as a condition that is congenital, or present from the time of birth (Jagose, 1996, p.22). Some resented the clinical connotations of the term homosexual, however, along with the apologetic attitude (Jagose, 1996, p.27) of the homophile movement. Gay identity thus emerged as an alternative to homosexual identity, and the gay liberation movement emerged as an alternative to the homophile movement.

Although it is an over-simplification, the Stonewall riots of 1969 are often cited as the beginning of the gay liberation movement. The Stonewall Inn was a New York gay and drag bar, predominately Black and Latino, and it was subject, like many gay bars at the time, to occasional police raids. These raids usually resulted in arrests for such forms of 'indecency' as dancing, kissing, and cross-dressing. When Stonewall was raided in the early morning hours of 28 June 1969, however, the patrons fought back, and they continued fighting all weekend. This sudden and unanimous expression of outrage is sometimes attributed to the death of gay icon Judy Garland,[2] whose funeral was held on 27 June 1969, but a more likely explanation is that these riots, as well as the gay liberation movement and other movements of the same era, including the women's liberation movement and the Black civil rights movement, were evidence of a growing sense of injustice in response to discrimination.[3]

This same sense of injustice eventually motivated an addition to the terminology associated with homosexual identity. Although 'gay' can be used in reference to women as well as men, the gay liberation movement was mainly concentrated on and directed toward gay men, and many lesbian women wanted the movement to recognize and include lesbian identity more explicitly. As a result of this demand, homosexual identity is usually referred to in terms of both lesbian identity and gay male identity. Unlike references to gay identity, which could include lesbian women, references to gay men and lesbian women are explicitly inclusive.

While more inclusive than 'gay', references to gay and lesbian identity do not reflect the full range of alternatives to heterosexuality. Given the popular misconception that bisexuality is a temporary identity that people eventually overcome, either by fully committing to homosexuality or by fully committing to heterosexuality, it is especially important to assert bisexuality as a sexual identity distinct from both heterosexuality and homosexuality. In order to encompass a broader range of identities and issues, references to alternative sexualities were expanded to include bisexual identity. A drawback of this expanded terminology is that it is longer and somewhat more awkward than referring to gay, or even gay and lesbian, identities. For this reason, the abbreviation GLB was introduced to refer to gay, lesbian, and bisexual identities. Recognizing that women always seem to come second, some people preferred to rearrange the order the letters, LGB, symbolically putting women ahead of men.

The recent addition of transgender identity completes a now familiar list, GLBT or LGBT. Unlike lesbian, gay, and bisexual, the category of transgender does not address sexual partner choice. Instead, it addresses the discrepancy some people experience between the biological sex category to which they were assigned and their identification as women or men. The inclusion of transgender people when accounting for alternative sexualities is not altogether arbitrary, however. Many who identify as lesbian, gay, or bisexual experience discrimination and violence for deviating from the heterosexual norm, and this is also the case for those who identify as transgender. Lesbian, gay, bisexual, and transgender identities all challenge the widespread expectation that biological females and biological males should exhibit the specific collection of attitudes and behaviours assigned to each sex category, and that they should partner sexually only with biological members of the opposite sex and corresponding gender categories.

The paradigm that initially established a deceptively simple distinction between homosexuality and heterosexuality has been expanded to encompass a broader range of people who deviate from the heterosexual norm. If this is sufficient to salvage the established paradigm, it will serve as an example of Kuhn's claim that some crises can be resolved by making adjustments to the paradigm. It will also serve as a reminder that 'The significance of crises is the indication they provide that an occasion for retooling has arrived' (Kuhn, 1970, p.76). If retooling is not sufficient to salvage the established paradigm, perhaps because the crisis is constituted by growing resentment over the very existence of the heterosexual norm, rather than by an easily corrected failure to name the various forms of deviance from that norm, then it will serve as an example of Kuhn's claim that some crises can be resolved only by a thoroughgoing revolution in which the existing paradigm is replaced by an alternative paradigm. Although it is impossible to know the outcome of the current crisis from the perspective of the present, adjustments to the established paradigm have thus far failed to resolve the crisis and have led, not to resolution or the promise thereof, but to further adjustments.

Recognizing that lesbian, gay, bisexual, and transgender identities, or LGBT identities, do not constitute an exhaustive or exclusive list of alternatives to the heterosexual norm, some amend the inventory by adding an additional category, such as 'questioning' or simply 'other'. The addition of the questioning category suggests that sexual identities develop over time, perhaps as the result of experimentation or exploration. The addition of the other category serves as a final attempt to cover any remaining sexual identities inadvertently omitted from the itemized list. In yet another effort to save the established paradigm, reference to alternative sexualities now refer to LGBTQ[4] or LGBTO identities. The crisis seems to be unfolding as quickly as adjustments to the paradigm can be made, however, and yet another mismatch between the paradigm and the human world reveals itself, this time in the form of intersex identity. Intersex, like transgender, does not address sexual partner choice and is not a sexual orientation in any strict sense. Nevertheless, intersex people and transgender people, like those who identify as lesbian, gay, and bisexual, violate the heterosexual norm. The heterosexual norm presupposes a distinction between biologically unproblematic women and biologically unproblematic men, and while transgender people render that distinction problematic by identifying as members of a different category than biology has assigned, intersex people render the distinction problematic because biology does not dictate a clear assignment to either sex category. The inclusion of intersex in the expanding inventory of alternative sexual identities, like the inclusion of transgender, therefore seems warranted. Those who have accepted this most recent attempt to save the established paradigm sometimes refer to LGBTQI identities, while others simply hope that LGBTO is sufficiently vague to eliminate the need for further additions.

Queer Theory

The ongoing need for such additions and adjustments may be an indication that the established paradigm can no longer be saved.

Despite expanding the range of recognized alternatives to normative heterosexuality, recent attempts to salvage the paradigm ultimately reinforce a binary model of human sexuality. The model is binary in at least two interrelated ways. First, it posits a social and sexual opposition between female and male, feminine and masculine.[5] Second, it posits a social and sexual opposition between forms of sexual expression that reinforce the allegedly complementary opposition between female and male, feminine and masculine, and forms of sexual expression that disrupt this opposition. In a more thoroughly revolutionary alternative to the established paradigm, *queer theory* avoids binary and hierarchical reasoning in general, and in connection with gender, sex, and sexuality in particular.[6] This is part of the reason why queer theory is notoriously difficult to define. In philosophy, a successful definition is often understood as an articulation of the necessary and sufficient conditions under which the term to be defined may be meaningfully and accurately applied. In other words, it draws an unproblematic boundary between the members of a given category and everything else, thereby participating in binary reasoning rather than transcending it. Queer theory, which trades essentialism and semantic atomism for social constructionism and semantic holism, recognizes that meaning is conveyed not by definitions of individual terms but by contextual relations between and among various terms. According to Jagose, 'Broadly speaking, queer describes those gestures or analytical models which dramatize incoherencies in the allegedly stable relations between chromosomal sex, gender and sexual desire' (Jagose, 1996, p.3). Although this is not a definition in the customary sense, it is an informative description nonetheless.[7]

Taken literally, queer describes something as unusual or unexpected, but it also has a history as a pejorative slur against those who violate – or are perceived as violating – the heterosexual norm. According to Halperin (2003), the pairing of the terms queer and theory is attributable to Teresa de Lauretis:

> Queer theory originally came into being as a joke. Teresa de Lauretis coined the phrase 'queer theory' to serve as the title of a conference that she held in February of 1990 at the University of California, Santa Cruz, where she is Professor of The History of Consciousness. She had heard the word 'queer' being tossed about in a gay-affirmative sense by activists, street kids, and members of the art world in New York during the late 1980s. She had the courage, and the conviction, to pair that scurrilous term with the academic holy word, 'theory.' Her usage was scandalously offensive. Sympathetic faculty at UCSC asked, in wounded tones, 'Why do they have to call it that?' But the conjunction was more than merely mischievous: it was deliberately disruptive.
>
> (2003, pp.339–40)

Called into existence in this manner, queer theory needed something to which it could now actually refer. Foucault's *The History of Sexuality, Volume 1* (1990), which was first published in the 1970s, along with Judith Butler's *Gender Trouble* (1990) and Eve Kosofsky Sedgwick's *The Epistemology of the Closet* (1990), which were published the same year that de Lauretis organized the first queer theory conference, are regarded by many as the seminal texts of queer theory. Written before the first documented use of the term queer theory, they nevertheless serve as early examples of the twofold attempt 'to unsettle the complacency of "lesbian and gay studies"' and 'to challenge the heterosexist underpinnings and assumptions of what conventionally passed for "theory" in academic circles' (Halperin, 2003, p.340).

Queer theory disrupts lesbian and gay studies, as well as women's studies, by avoiding binary contrasts between female and male, feminine and masculine, homosexual and heterosexual, and so on. Nevertheless, queer theory is compatible with the existence of female and male identities, butch and femme identities, homosexual and heterosexual identities, transgender identities, and various other identities that exist, be it comfortably or uncomfortably, within the binary system. Quite simply, queer theory does not dictate the eradication of existing categories of gender, sex, and sexuality, though many people assume that it must. Within queer theory, what is sometimes described as a rejection of binary contrasts is perhaps better described as social constructionism with respect to those contrasts. Recall that essentialism is the belief that various identity categories, such as female and male, feminine and masculine, homosexual and heterosexual, reflect innate characteristics that comprise the fundamental nature of the members of those categories, whereas social constructionism is the belief that such identity categories are historical and cultural developments. This does not necessarily mean that they have no empirical basis, but it does mean that the categories are empirically underdetermined. Recall that underdetermination occurs when empirical evidence alone provides an insufficient basis for choosing one paradigm over another.

The concept of underdetermination is easier to demonstrate than it is to explain. Suppose that you have been given the task of articulating a basis for group inclusion or exclusion when presented with a set of unique individuals.[8] When presented, for example, with images of four shapes (see Figure 3.1), three unshaded and one shaded, it would make sense to designate shading as the relevant criterion for category inclusion. At the same time, however, if three of the shapes are rounded and one consists of angled edges (see Figure 3.1), it would likewise make sense to designate roundness as the relevant criterion. Although there is an empirically observable difference between shaded and unshaded figures, and between rounded and angled figures, nothing empirical dictates reference to these features when determining which individuals belong to the set and which individuals do not. Similarly, when presented with images of four arrows (see Figure 3.2), three of which are the same colour, three of which point in the same direction, and three of which are the same size, the decision to base category membership on colour, direction, or size is empirically underdetermined.

Figure 3.1 Shapes for categorization challenge

Which one of these things is not like the others?

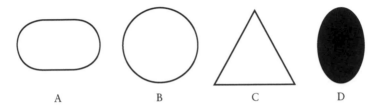

A   B   C   D

Figure 3.2 Arrows for categorization challenge

Which one of these things is not like the others?

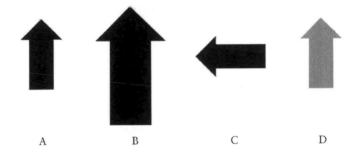

A   B   C   D

Although the selection criteria for designating some things as different from other things may be empirically underdetermined, the categories created by these designations have real implications. If grey arrows were victims of violence or large arrows were denied job opportunities because of their perceived deviation from category standards, the observation that category standards are socially constructed would not eliminate their impact on those wayward arrows. Similarly, the recognition that the standards established by contemporary western categories of gender, sex, and sexuality are socially constructed does not eliminate the impact of these categories. It does, however, serve as an invitation to construct alternative categories. The goal is not to exchange one empirically underdetermined set of categories for another empirically underdetermined set of categories. Instead, the goal is the proliferation and multiplication of categories. One way to challenge a binary opposition is to deny or ignore the distinction it identifies, for example by denying or ignoring the distinction between feminine and masculine. Unfortunately, this approach ignores the significance of this distinction for many people, including many who identify as lesbian, gay, bisexual, or transgender. Yet another way to challenge a binary opposition is to expand the range of alternatives, trading duality for multiplicity. By challenging the binary in this manner, queer theory is capable of resisting essentialism while simultaneously affirming the experiences of people for whom the established categories are problematic as well as of people for whom the established categories are unproblematic.

Recognizing that sexuality is unique to each individual person, it is difficult to believe that there is anyone whose sexuality is not unusual, unexpected, or somehow queer. It therefore makes sense to regard as queer even some people who might otherwise be expected to identify as heterosexual. The point of this shift is not to allow heterosexuals to claim homosexual identities if they decide they can gain some advantage by doing so. Instead, the point is to shift the balance of power, at least symbolically, by acknowledging that far more of us are queer than not. But queer theory is not just about increased inclusion. It is also about the constant need to acknowledge that, while categories may be useful, perhaps even necessary, for understanding oneself and relating with others, no particular category or set of categories is itself necessary, and even the most deeply entrenched categories are subject to revision.

Additional Resources

- Kuhn, T. S. (1970). 'Chapter X: Revolutions as changes of world view', *The Structure of Scientific Revolutions*, pp.111–35. Chicago: University of Chicago Press.
- Sedgwick, E. K. (1990). 'The epistemology of the closet', *The Epistemology of the Closet*, pp. 67–90. Berkeley: University of California Press.
- Halperin, D. M. (2003). 'The normalization of queer theory'. *Journal of Homosexuality, 45*(2–4), 339–43.
- Hall, R. (1990). *The Well of Loneliness: A 1920s Classic of Lesbian Fiction.* New York: Anchor Books.

References

Baum, L. F. (2005). *15 Books in 1: L. Frank Baum's Original 'Oz' Series.* Shoes and Ships and Sealing Wax, Ltd. (original works published 1908–20).
Butler, J. (1990). *Gender Trouble: Feminism and the Subversion of Identity.* New York: Routledge.

Carter, D. (2004). *Stonewall: The Riots That Sparked the Gay Revolution*. New York: St Martin's Press.

Foucault, M. (1990). *The History of Sexuality, Volume 1: An Introduction* (R. Hurley, trans.). New York: Vintage Books (original work published in French in 1976).

Hall, R. (1990). *The Well of Loneliness: A 1920s Classic of Lesbian Fiction*. New York: Anchor Books (original work published in 1928).

Halperin, D. M. (2003). 'The normalization of queer theory'. *Journal of Homosexuality*, 45(2–4), 339–43.

Jagose, A. (1996). *Queer Theory: An Introduction*. New York: NYU Press.

Kuhn, T. S. (1970). *The Structure of Scientific Revolutions*. Chicago: University of Chicago Press (original work published in 1962).

Marinucci, M. (2005, Spring). 'GLBT (and sometimes Q)'. *The F-word Ezine*. Retrieved from http://www.thef-wordzine.com/lgbt_terms505.html

Marx, K. (1970). 'Theses on Feuerbach'. In K. Marx and F. Engels, *The German Ideology, Part One, with Selections from Parts Two and Three and Supplementary Texts* (C. J. Arthur, ed.). New York: International Publishers (original work published posthumously in 1888).

Sedgwick, E. K. (1990). 'The epistemology of the closet', *The Epistemology of the Closet*, pp.67–90. Berkeley: University of California Press.

Notes

1 Portions of this discussion of sexual identity categories were included in the article 'GLBT (and sometimes Q)' (Marinucci, 2005).

2 Judy Garland, who played the role of Dorothy in *The Wizard of Oz*, has been a gay icon since the 1950s, and the phrase 'friend of Dorothy' is sometimes used as an informal reference to gay men.

3 For a historical account of the Stonewall riots and surrounding events, refer to David Carter's *Stonewall: The Riots That Sparked the Gay Revolution*.

4 In some cases, the Q in LGBTQ or GLBTQ does not represent questioning, but instead represents queer, which is discussed in more detail in the next section of this chapter.

5 The binary opposition actually extends much further, and includes contrasts between body and mind, nature and culture, emotion and intellect, passivity and action, and so on. This establishes a link between the feminine and the body, nature, emotion, passivity, etc., which has consequences for members of groups that, for reasons unrelated to gender, sex, or sexuality, are associated with the body, nature, emotion, or passivity. Consider, for example, the cultural stereotypes that assume a connection between Native American people and nature, between Latin American people and emotion, between people with physical disabilities and passivity.

6 Although the concepts of gender, sex, and sexuality are interrelated, it is often useful to differentiate among them. Gender usually refers to constellations of characteristics commonly regarded as feminine and masculine, while sex usually refers to constellations of characteristics commonly regarded as female and male. While gender is generally believed to be socially acquired, sex is generally believed to be biologically innate. As addressed in a later chapter,

this account downplays the many complexities surrounding the biology of sex. Finally, sexuality usually refers to intimate practices, especially those related to the selection of intimate partners, and there is widespread disagreement about whether sexuality is socially acquired or biologically innate.

7 Those already familiar with postmodernism might also benefit from the overly simplified but potentially explanatory description of queer theory as a postmodern interpretation of gender, sex, and sexuality.

8 This challenge was inspired by a recurring segment and corresponding jingle from the classic children's television series *Sesame Street*, which posed the question 'Which one of these things is not like the others?'.

SEX

'Tell me,' said the Patchwork Girl earnestly, 'do all those queer people you mention really live in the Land of Oz?'

(L. Frank Baum, *The Patchwork Girl of Oz*, p.278)

4

Unwelcome Interventions

*They wakened the boy at daybreak, the Scarecrow saying to him:
'We have discovered something queer, and therefore we must
counsel together what to do about it.'*
(L. Frank Baum, *The Tin Woodman of Oz*, p.500)

Parsing the Sexes

The term sex is used in at least two distinct but related ways. It sometimes makes reference to the sex categories into which people are organized, as conveyed by such expressions as 'the female sex' and 'the male sex'. At other times, however, it makes reference to the various activities commonly recognized as sex acts, as conveyed by such expressions as 'vaginal sex' and 'oral sex', as well as the familiar but oddly limiting phrase, '*the* sex act'. Etymologically, 'sex' derives from the same root as the word 'section', as in to parse into sections. Taken from the Latin 'sexus', it refers literally to division. Many words divide the world, or some part of it, into separate categories. Indeed, most, perhaps even all, nouns perform this function by differentiating between what belongs inside the category to which the noun refers and what lies outside its boundaries. Unlike most other nouns, however, the term 'sex' makes direct reference to the process of parsing the world, and this carries an implicit suggestion that the way in which 'sex' parses the world is of utmost significance. It is not just *any* parsing; rather, it is a parsing that, at least in the English language, is acknowledged as *the* parsing. Moreover, the dual usage of the single term 'sex' to refer both to what a someone is (in the case of sex categories) and also to what someone does (in the case of sex acts) betrays the underlying assumption that, when it comes to sex, what someone is determines what that person does and that, by the same token, what someone does is the ultimate expression of what that person is at the most fundamental level.

Sex category membership is usually regarded as a biological condition. For the most part, contemporary science acknowledges two basic sex categories, female and male. Genitals, gonads, chromosomes, and hormones are the main criteria by which specific people are categorized as members of either sex. Genitals, gonads, chromosomes, and hormones are most often aligned such that the genitals, gonads, chromosomes, and hormones of any one person usually fit neatly into exactly one of the two sex categories. The biological archetype of the human female is someone with a clearly recognizable vagina (with no genital structure that resembles a penis) and a uterus (with no structures that resemble testicles), as well as an XX chromosome pattern and hormone levels that are within the range designated as normal for women. The male standard includes a penis (but no vaginal structure) and testicles (but no ovaries), along with an XY chromosome pattern and hormone levels similar to those found in other males.

Judgments about the sex of other people usually come easily, and with remarkable accuracy considering that most ordinary situations do not provide opportunities to examine the genitals, gonads, chromosomes, or hormones of others. Observable secondary sex characteristics, such as the presence or relative absence of facial hair and the presence or relative absence of breast tissue, provide some clues, but they do not always provide adequate or accurate information. While many biologically unambiguous males are unable to achieve a significant growth of facial hair, many biologically unambiguous females devote an inordinate amount of time and money to the task of removing it. There is likewise considerable variability in the amount of breast tissue with which people are endowed, regardless of whether they are female or male. Secondary sex characteristics and other observable bodily features can be misleading. Despite a general tendency for males to be larger, hairier, and more muscular than females, particular females are occasionally larger, hairier, and more muscular than particular males.

Given that biological criteria for determining sex are not publicly accessible and secondary sex characteristics are not always reliable, it is remarkable that there is not more confusion when it comes to separating people on the basis of sex. The ease with which most people can be recognized as female or male has less to do with their biology than it has to do with various social markers. Although anyone, female or male, can wear a dress or a short hairstyle, such social displays are fairly reliable unless people consciously present themselves in an ambiguous manner, which is sometimes referred to informally as *genderfucking*. When people make an earnest attempt to style themselves *as* women or to style themselves *as* men, however, there is rarely any doubt about which category they mean to embody – even if others do no approve of their effort, as is often the case when those who are biologically female style themselves as men or when those who are biologically male style themselves as women.

It is ironic that, despite the tendency within contemporary western culture to think of the X and Y chromosomes as the *sine qua non*[1] of sex differentiation, this is the one feature that is perhaps the least likely to be confirmed in most people. Furthermore, even when genetic testing is available, the sex category to which someone belongs is sometimes still unclear. There are some people in whom the genitals, gonads, chromosomes, or hormones are in disagreement or are themselves so ambiguous that not even the medical experts agree about the best way to categorize them. Some people appear female despite having the XY chromosome pattern associated with males. People with androgen insensitivity syndrome, for example, have both X and Y chromosomes, but their bodies do not respond to male hormones, or androgens. As a result, they usually have physical features, including genitals, that are more readily recognizable as female than male.

The relationship between hormones and sex is complicated by the fact that women and men produce the same hormones. It is only the amount of certain hormones, specifically oestrogens and androgens, that varies according to sex. This means that there is no precise boundary between normal and abnormal hormone levels for women and men:

> Men and women produce the same kinds of hormones, though usually in different relative quantities, but we know that all girls' and women's bodies do not uniformly produce a single identifiable 'feminine' cocktail of hormones, nor do all boys and men produce a single, identifiable sort of 'masculine' cocktail. To use hormones as a dividing line we would have to decide where to draw the boundaries of acceptable hormonal variations on malehood and femalehood.
>
> (Dreger 1998b, p.7)

It can be difficult to differentiate between a large clitoris and a small penis, and assignment as male or female is sometimes a judgment call. This is likewise the case for people endowed with testes or partial testes as well as a uterus or partial uterus. It is the case once again for people who do not have a straightforward XX or XY chromosome pattern, but instead have an XXY, XYY, or XXX pattern, or a even mosaic pattern in which some cells in the body are XX and others are XY. In other words, there are exceptions and ambiguities regardless of whether sex is understood to be a function of genitals, gonads, chromosomes, or hormones.

For a very public example of the problematic use of chromosomes as the basis for sex differentiation, consider recent discussions regarding the International Olympic Committee's (IOC) use of what has been dubbed 'gender testing', but which would more precisely be identified as 'sex testing' or, even more precisely, as 'sex chromosome testing'

(Kolata, 1992; Saner, 2008). Testing was first performed in 1968. Since that time, 'two or three women have failed the test at virtually every Olympic competition and been disqualified for life' (Kolata, 1992). It is unfortunate that, as far as most of these competitors knew, they were just ordinary women who happened to be extraordinary athletes. To avoid such incidents, the IOC discontinued universal testing:

> At the Atlanta games in 1996, eight female athletes failed sex tests but were all cleared on appeal; seven were found to have an 'intersex' condition. As a result, by the time of the Sydney games in 2000, the IOC had abolished universal sex testing but, as will happen in Beijing, some women still had to prove they really were women.
>
> (Saner, 2008)

According to the Intersex Society of North America (ISNA), intersex refers to a range of exceptions to the expected alignment of genitals, gonads, chromosomes, and hormones into exactly two distinct sex categories, female and male.

> 'Intersex' is a general term used for a variety of conditions in which a person is born with a reproductive or sexual anatomy that doesn't seem to fit the typical definitions of female or male. For example, a person might be born appearing to be female on the outside, but having mostly male-typical anatomy on the inside. Or a person may be born with genitals that seem to be in-between the usual male and female types – for example, a girl may be born with a noticeably large clitoris, or lacking a vaginal opening, or a boy may be born with a notably small penis, or with a scrotum that is divided so that it has formed more like labia. Or a person may be born with mosaic genetics, so that some of her cells have XX chromosomes and some of them have XY.
>
> (ISNA, n.d.)

Such exceptions are rare, but they are more common than many people realize. According to most official estimates, intersex conditions occur somewhere between one in 1500 and one in 2000 births (ISNA, n.d.), but there is at least some degree of genital ambiguity in about one in 100 births (Thomas, 2005). Things are thus complicated by the fact that there is little consensus about what constitutes a person who is intersex and what constitutes a person who is unproblematically female or unproblematically male (ISNA, n.d.).

Sex and Science

Because different criteria can be applied to determine sex in questionable cases, there is room in particular instances for disagreement about whether a specific individual is biologically intersex, biologically female, or biologically male. There is also room for disagreement about what it means to introduce intersex as a third sex category. For some, intersex constitutes a natural kind category on a par with the two well-established sex categories, female and male. To illustrate, consider an analogy with hair colour. Although dark- and fair-haired people are far more common than those with red hair worldwide, mainstream science does not therefore regard red hair as a failed attempt by nature to produce hair of a more common colour. Although a similar perspective could be applied to the phenomenon of intersex, some instead regard intersex as an unfortunate aberration. Again, consider an analogy with hair colour. Where red hair is included in the range of what mainstream science regards as normal, the lack of pigmentation characteristic of albinism is not. Instead, it is attributed to an intrusion upon the processes through which the body normally produces melanin, just as intersex is sometimes attributed to an interruption or disruption in the processes that normally produce the more familiar alignment of unambiguous genital, gonadal, hormonal, and chromosomal structures. While the accepted paradigm precludes speculation regarding the hair colour a redhead 'should have had' or 'would have had', it invites such speculation regarding people with albinism.

Depending on the paradigm, otherwise healthy intersex people are regarded either as imperfect specimens of one of the two well-established sex categories, or as unproblematic members of some alternative sex category. Scientists have not reached consensus about which paradigm to apply to the phenomenon of intersex. Even those who agree that human sex differentiation is not limited to the categories of female and male do not always agree about the number of natural kinds into which human sex divides. Ann Fausto-Sterling (1993), for example, makes a compelling case for organizing the biological concept of sex into, not two or three, but a minimum of five distinct categories. As demonstrated by Alice Domurat Dreger (1998b), ideas about the status of alternative sex categories have undergone some significant changes throughout recent history:

> The literature on hermaphroditism also reveals, however, that there was not a single, unified medical opinion about which traits should count as essentially or significantly feminine or masculine. In France and Britain, the sexes were constructed in many different, sometimes conflicting ways in hermaphrodite theory and medical practice, as medical men struggled to come up with a system of sex difference that would hold. Ultimately it was not only the

hermaphrodite's body that lay ensconced in ambiguity, but medical and scientific concepts of the male and female as well. We see here not stagnant ideas about sex, but vibrant, growing, struggling theories. Sex itself was still open to doubt.

(Dreger, 1998b, p.16)

Although there is a movement underway in North America to promote awareness about and acceptance of intersex identities, the medical profession remains committed to the use of surgical and hormonal intervention in intersex patients:

Scientific dogma has held fast to the assumption that without medical care hermaphrodites are doomed to a life of misery. Yet there are few empirical studies to back up that assumption, and some of the same research gathered to build a case for medical treatment contradicts it.

(Fausto-Sterling, 1993, p.23)

There is often a great deal of shame surrounding intersex identity and secrecy surrounding surgical and hormonal interventions performed by the medical profession. Children who are born intersex often discover this only after they are adults, and often only by accident. Some intersex adults lament the loss of the bodies and identities they might have developed had they not been subjected to medical intervention (Ward, 2000). As a result of this intervention, they no longer have the bodies they were born with, nor, however, do they have bodies that are unproblematically female or male.

For a particularly poignant example of the arrogance with which the medical profession has been known to impose itself on the sexed body in the interest of regulation, consider the well-known case of Bruce, aka Brenda, aka David Reimer.[2] Bruce Reimer, who was identified at birth as biologically male, was surgically reassigned as female following a botched circumcision. Bruce was renamed Brenda and raised as a girl. Bruce's identical twin brother, Brian, suffered no complications and was raised as a boy. Because the two children were identical twins, this case was regarded by many as an opportunity to empirically test the theory that the distinction between women and men is primarily attributable to socialization. Initially, Brenda's reassignment was believed to be so successful that the 'twins case' was cited in many women's studies textbooks as evidence of gender socialization.[3] Apparently, however, Brenda never felt completely comfortable as a girl and eventually resumed a male identity, this time under the name David Reimer. Sadly, Reimer never found peace and finally committed suicide in 2004.

In an article for *Ms. Magazine*, 'Making the Cut', Martha Coventry (2000) outlines the recent history of the medical manipulation of bodies in the interest of sexual control. The story begins in Victorian England with the theory, attributed to a medical doctor by the name of Isaac Baker Brown, that clitoral stimulation was the source of a variety of health problems in women. Extreme cases of conditions ranging from epilepsy to the amorphous diagnosis of hysteria, were treated with clitoridectomy. By the middle of the 20th century, there was a fairly widespread recognition that clitoridectomy was ineffective both at preventing female masturbation and at treating the various conditions to which female masturbation had been linked. The procedure was not, therefore, abandoned. Instead, it was simply redirected toward cosmetic ends. The new theory, attributed to a doctor by the name of John Money, is that an enlarged clitoris can be trimmed, and thereby normalized, for improved quality of life.

In a sidebar titled 'The Unabridged Version', Coventry relates a story that reveals the oversized clitoris to be a potential source of pleasure:

> Some girls born with big clitorises are not surgically altered. Perhaps no one notices their clitoris at birth, or maybe they are born at home away from medical intervention. Kim is a petite 26-year-old whose clitoris is large enough when erect to penetrate her women lovers. She has never had any shame about it. 'I really didn't have a problem with it. I mean, people didn't go around looking between my legs. It wasn't something I had to hide, because no one looked at it. I was much more concerned about other things, like my thighs being fat.' She remembers that growing up 'anything I rubbed on was very sexual to me. My clitoris was big enough to have a very satisfying experience; most of it was outside my labia.' But Kim, a mother with a child of her own, still worries about what the medical establishment could do to her. She jokes only half-heartedly of getting a medical ID bracelet that reads, 'In case of accident, DO NOT remove clitoris'.
>
> (Coventry, 2000, p.58)

Despite what medical practitioners think about the potential quality of life for a woman with a large clitoris, Kim's story is a compelling case in favour of allowing those born with ambiguous but otherwise healthy genitals to wait until puberty or adulthood to make their own informed decisions about whether to pursue surgery. Kim's story also serves as a reminder that when it comes to sex, as noted by Milton Diamond (in Thomas, 2005), 'Variation is the norm. Biology loves difference. Society hates it.'

Sex Acts

In addition to the use of 'sex' to refer to sex categories, there is also a usage in which 'sex' refers to sexual activity. Because biology seeks to explain, among other things, such processes as mating and reproduction, biological definitions of sex categories typically make reference to sexuality, while biological definitions of sexual activity, in turn, make reference to sex categories. The fact that the same word, 'sex', is used in reference both to sex categories and to sexual activity reveals an underlying assumption that sex, in terms of sexual activity, derives directly from the division into sex categories and that sex, in terms of sex categories, leads directly to sexual activity. In the strictly biological sense, sex categories and sex acts are intimately connected, and both are ultimately concerned with reproduction. In practice, however, neither sex categories nor sex acts involve reproduction much of the time. The experience of living as a woman or a man often has little, if anything, to do with the production of offspring. Likewise, the experience of participating in sex acts often has very little, if anything, to do with the production of offspring. Even the intimacy that occurs between those involved in monogamous pair bonds that carry the potential to produce children is not always directed toward the end goal of reproduction. Nevertheless, there seems to be an implicit assumption by many people that there is an invisible but essential link between sex categories, sex acts, and reproduction. But just as there are some people who do not fit easily into either of the binary sex categories, there are also people who break the expected continuity between membership in one sex category and sexual desire that is oriented toward members of the contrasting sex category for reproductive ends. Consider, for example, biological women who are drawn toward sexuality with other biological women, and biological men who are drawn toward sexuality with other biological men, such that reproduction as a direct consequence of the sex acts they perform together is simply not possible. Also consider those for whom the sex category of others is irrelevant in determining sexual desire, such that reproduction is possible, but not a necessary consequence of the sex acts in which they participate. Consider those for whom sexual desire is devoid of any procreative drive, such that reproduction is an unwanted potential consequence of some sex acts, but not its purpose. Consider the many reasons for which the alleged connection between sex, sexuality, and reproduction is absent for most people at most times.

Sex is sufficiently complex to defy easy definition. Indeed, just what to include as examples of sex acts is open to debate and often depends on context. The boundaries of sexual desire and sexual behaviour are often unclear, and there is no single, authoritative set of necessary and sufficient conditions by which sex acts are defined. What constitutes a sex act in one context may be decidedly non-sexual in a different context. This is evident in the difference, for example, between hugging or kissing a friend and hugging or kissing a lover. It is also evident in the difference between activities that people do not usually regard as erotic, and those same activities when performed by people for whom they have taken on erotic significance. Virtually any ordinary activity could, at least in principle, be rendered erotic under the right circumstances, and virtually any erotic activity could, in principle, be rendered ordinary. Is it properly regarded as a sex act when someone wears leather, rubber, silk, lace, fishnet stockings, stiletto heels, work boots, a maid's uniform, a school uniform, an animal costume, or any other garment around which a fetish might be formed? Is it properly regarded as a sex act when someone steps in ground meat? Does the answer depend on whether this is done to satisfy the sexual urges of oneself or a partner? Does masturbation constitute a sex act? Does the answer depend on whether another person is present? That there seems to be no end to such questions casts doubt on the possibility of articulating an exhaustive and exclusive list of necessary and sufficient conditions for distinguishing between sex acts and other sorts of acts.

Sex lacks boundaries in that there is a seemingly limitless array of potential sex acts. For at least some people, sex lacks boundaries in another way as well. While sexual pleasure, particularly the sexual pleasure of men, is often characterized in terms of the single, discrete moment of ejaculation, some people, particularly some women, describe sexual pleasure as a more continuous experience. According to Luce Irigaray, for example, a woman's sexual pleasure is not confined to a single body part, but rather 'the geography of her pleasure is far more diversified, more multiple in its differences, more complex, more subtle, than is commonly imagined' (Irigaray, 1985, p.28). Irigaray explains the impact of this 'geography' of women's pleasure:

> Thus what they desire is precisely nothing, and at the same time everything. Always something more and something else besides that *one* – sexual organ, for example – that you give them, attribute to them. Their desire is often interpreted, and feared, as a sort of insatiable hunger, a voracity that will swallow you whole. Whereas it really involves a different economy more than anything else, one that upsets the linearity of a project, undermines the goal-object of a desire, diffuses the polarization toward a single pleasure, disconcerts fidelity to a single discourse...
> (Irigaray, 1985, pp.29–30) [ellipses in original]

In the final analysis, biology alone is insufficient to divide the human population into women and men, and it is likewise insufficient to establish our pleasures and desires. The unique sexuality of any person in particular is not a straightforward consequence of membership in a given sex category. This does not mean, however, that sex and sexuality do not have a biological component, nor does it mean that sex and sexuality are completely unconnected with reproduction. Perhaps this is best explained by extending the earlier analogy with hair colour a bit further. Hair colour, like sex, is something that is usually thought of as a biological condition. In addition, hair colour, like sex, is often simplified into two categories. Hair can be divided into just light or blond shades and dark or brunette shades, despite the recognition that there is variation within these two categories, as in the case of hair that is platinum blond, dirty blond, chestnut, raven, etc., and in the case of hair that does not fall into either of the two dominant categories, as in the case of hair that is copper, auburn, etc. Hair colour is unlike sex, however, in that people are usually comfortable with a lack of certainty about adult hair colour at the time of birth. Bald infants usually grow hair, light-haired children often become dark-haired adults, and people accept that hair colour can change even during adult life, as through greying or whitening of the hair. In other words, although hair colour is understood to be a biological trait, it is not thereby regarded as stable throughout life. In addition, cosmetic intervention enables people to change their hair colour with relative ease. Such intervention sometimes invites questions about authenticity, as expressed through questions along the lines of, 'Is that a *natural* blond?'. Even so, cosmetic intervention with regard to hair colour is more commonly understood as a matter of aesthetic preference or creative expression. Those who favour 'letting nature run its course' and 'aging gracefully' tend not to devote much effort to preventing others from making cosmetic changes – and when they do, it is generally for reasons other than a belief in the primary importance of hair colour: for example, some feminists might be inclined to discourage women from attempting to conform to a culturally accepted standard of beauty that displays a preference for youthful blonds.

Thus, the mere fact that sex is biological does not establish that sex is fixed at birth or stable throughout life. It is entirely possible that, just as hair colour sometimes undergoes both voluntary and involuntary changes throughout a person's life, so too does sex. Both the sex category to which a person belongs and the sex acts in which a person is likely to participate can undergo changes throughout life. Although it seems obvious that even very young children are sexual beings, how they enact their sexuality is presumably quite different than it will be when they are older. The fact that sex is biological is likewise insufficient to establish that sex is always beyond the realm of personal choice. Just as hair colour can undergo elective changes throughout life, so can the various features associated with sex category membership. The purpose of this analogy is not to suggest that people are as whimsical about changing sex category as they often are about changing hair colour. Instead, it is simply to acknowledge that biological features can and often do change over the course of the human lifespan.[4]

Additional Resources

- Kolata, G. (1992). 'Who is female? Science can't say'. *The New York Times.* 16 February 1992.
- Saner, E. (2008). 'The gender trap'. *The Guardian.* 30 July 2008.
- Fausto-Sterling, A. (1993). 'The five sexes: Why male and female are not enough'. *The Sciences, 33*(2), 20–25.
- Dreger, A. D. (1998). '"Ambiguous sex" – Or ambivalent medicine? Ethical issues in the treatment of intersexuality'. *The Hastings Center Report, 28*(3), 24–35.
- Coventry, M. (2000). 'Making the cut'. *Ms. Magazine, 10*(6), 52–60.
- Colapinto, J. (1997). 'The case of John/Joan'. *Rolling Stone.* 11 December 1997, 54–97.
- Thomas, A. (2005). *Middle Sexes: Redefining He and She.* HBO Documentary Films.

References

Baum, L. F. (2005). *15 Books in 1: L. Frank Baum's Original 'Oz' series.* Shoes and Ships and Sealing Wax, Ltd. (Original works published 1908–20).

Colapinto, J. (1997). 'The case of John/Joan'. *Rolling Stone,* 11 December 1997, 54–97.

Colapinto, J. (2000). *As Nature Made Him: The Boy Who Was Raised as a Girl.* New York: Perennial.

Coventry, M. (2000). 'Making the cut'. *Ms. magazine, 10*(6), 52–60.

Dreger, A. D. (1998a). '"Ambiguous sex" – Or ambivalent medicine? Ethical issues in the treatment of intersexuality'. *The Hastings Center Report, 28*(3), 24–35.

Dreger, A. D. (1998b). *Hermaphrodites and the Medical Invention of Sex.* Cambridge MA: Harvard University Press.

Fausto-Sterling, A. (1993). 'The five sexes: Why male and female are not enough'. *The Sciences, 33*(2), 20–25.

Intersex Society of North America (n.d.). *Frequently Asked Questions.* Retrieved 27 March 27 2010, from http://www.isna.org/faq/what_is_intersex

Irigaray, L. (1985). 'This sex which is not one'. In *This Sex Which Is Not One* (C. Porter, trans.), pp.23–33. Ithaca: Cornell University Press (original work published in French in 1977).

Kolata, G. (1992). 'Who is female? Science can't say'. *The New York Times.* 16 February 1992.

Saner, E. (2008). 'The gender trap'. *The Guardian.* 30 July 2008.

Thomas, A. (2005). *Middle Sexes: Redefining He and She.* HBO Documentary Films.

Ward, P. (2000). *Is It a Boy or a Girl?* Great Falls VA: Discovery Channel.

Notes

1 *Sine qua non* is a Latin expression that designates an essential condition.
2 For an account of Reimer's life that is quite moving, though not completely free of sexist undertones, refer to John Colapinto's *As Nature Made Him: The Boy Who was Raised as a Girl* (2000).
3 As discussed in Section III, gender is usually contrasted with sex as a way to refer to the socially acquired characteristics by which women and men are differentiated.
4 The process of transitioning into sex categories other than those assigned at birth is discussed in more detail in Chapter 5.

5

Welcome Transformations

*'I've seen queer things since I came to the Land of Oz,' said he,
'but never anything queerer than this band of adventurers. Let us
sit down a while, and have a talk and get acquainted.'*
(L. Frank Baum, *The Patchwork Girl of Oz*, p.274)

Women-Born Women

In 1976, sisters Linda and Kristie Vogel, along with their friend Mary
Kindig, organized a summer concert in Hart, Michigan, featuring music
by and for women. The concert was so successful that it became an
annual event, now known as the Michigan Womyn's Music Festival,[1]
or less formally, 'Michfest' or even just 'Michigan', and abbreviated
throughout as MWMF. As indicated in a promotional flyer from 1978,
the festival was conceived as 'A Gathering of Mothers and Daughters
for Womyn-Born Womyn' (Vogel, 2000). According to Linda Vogel,
'The hallmark of Michigan has always been its creation of separate,
self-defined and deeply honored womyn's space' (Vogel, 2000). The
festival grounds, often referred to simply as 'the land', are designated
exclusively for women, which reflects a commitment to the separatist
agenda associated with some versions of radical feminism.

Briefly, radical feminism is characterized by a critique of patriarchal
oppression, often coupled with the belief that patriarchal oppression
is inevitable in virtually any social context that puts women and men
together.[2] According to a 1975 document issued by Oven Productions,
women-only concert venues provide a welcome alternative to the
ubiquitous sexism of the larger US culture:

Because of women's past experiences in a sexist society, men
(regardless of their politics, consciousness and good intentions)
negatively alter the dynamic of a woman-space. Men represent our
oppression...sexism. For women who have been raped, beaten,
deserted, fired, misled, manipulated, discriminated against, had

their children taken away, etc. the man at the concert may trigger
pain, even if he is the nicest guy in town. We want women's concerts
to be the most open, unoppressive, liberating possible. We do not
always succeed, but womenspace free of real and/or symbolic
oppression can have a monumental effect on women. Men who
really understand sexism are supportive of this concept. In fact,
they do not want to put themselves in the situation of representing
the oppressor at a women's event.

(Oven Productions, 1975) [ellipses in original]

The document also suggests that those who demand a defence of women-
only spaces ultimately, though perhaps inadvertently, drain energy from
the women who seek them:

It is also important that men not drain women of energy by constantly
demanding explanation after explanation. The government keeps
activists tied up in trials (their money, their energy, their friends)
in order to keep them from continuing their important work. Men
often do this to women. This kind of energy drain is a subtle and
dangerous form of sexism. There are lots of books, records, etc.
which deal with women's struggles. Men can investigate these
resources.

(Oven Productions, 1975)

The women-only policy at MWMF was introduced in an effort to
resist and respond to sexist oppression. In 1991, however, controversy
exploded around this policy when it was used to evict Nancy Burkholder,
a male-to-female (MTF) transgender person, or trans woman, from the
festival grounds.[3]

'Trans' is often used to indicate transgender or transsexual identity.
There are some people whose sense of self is inconsistent with their
assignment as female or male, even when that assignment is biologically
unproblematic. There are biologically unambiguous females who
nevertheless identify as men, and vice-versa. That such discrepancies
are even possible reveals a gap between biological definitions of sex and
the broader definitions of what it means to be a woman or a man. The
concept of gender is used in reference to the various connotations and
expectations that are associated with biological sex but are not contained
within the biological definitions.[4] More recently, however, many people
have begun using gender almost interchangeably with sex. For some
people, this shift reflects an understanding of the ways in which biological
sex is itself complicated, as well, perhaps, as a desire to be inclusive of
those for whom there is a significant incongruity between the sex of
the body and the internal experience of feminine or masculine identity.
Indeed, the term transgender has largely replaced the term transsexual in

reference to people who opt for medical intervention to bring the sex of the body into closer alignment with their internal identity.[5] In addition, transgender is a broader term, which also includes those who experience this sort of incongruence and express their internal identity without medical assistance.

Many people, including many transsexual and transgender people, opposed the woman-born-woman requirement for entry into the MWMF:

> As you know, the Michigan Women's Music Festival has a policy of denying the entrance of anyone who is not a woman-born-woman. This definition excludes transgendered people. This policy is transphobia in its most insidious forms. It divides the women's community into 'real women' and 'kinda-women' and wastes valuable resources that could be used fighting for things that benefit all women.
>
> (BethX, 1999)

The women-born-women requirement excluded trans women, and outrage over this exclusion led to the creation of Camp Trans.[6] Initially conceived as a protest site following Nancy Burkholder's 1991 eviction from the festival grounds, Camp Trans waned within a few years, but re-emerged in 1999 as an alternative festival venue existing alongside MWMF, offering workshops on and gaining support for trans inclusion.

Less obvious than the exclusion of trans women was the simultaneous exclusion, or at least alienation, of anyone unwilling or unable to identify as a woman-born-woman:

> Genderqueer people and others who identify as neither male or female are also excluded under this policy even if they were raised as girls. In 2000, several 'trannie boys, boydykes, FTMs, Lesbian Avengers and young gender-variant women' – who were not transsexual women – were evicted from the festival for their refusal to identify as 'womyn-born womyn' either because they no longer identify as women, or in solidarity with their comrades.
>
> (Koyama, FAQ, n.d.)

Many feminists in general, along with many MWMF attendees in particular, prefer policies and practices of inclusion over policies and practices of exclusion. According to the text of a 2001 petition against MWMF's women-born-women policy:

> Many of us have had to face discrimination and harassment because of our gender expression, and we see the scapegoating of

trans-women as part of the same cycle of violence. Whether we're harassed because we 'don't look like women' or we 'look like we're asking for it,' it's all a part of the same sexist, gender-rigid, patriarchal system that we are trying to resist.

(Lamm *et al.*, 2001)

In the words of Riki Wilchins, as quoted in a 1999 press release by Clare Howell, 'Discrimination against any woman must always be contested' (Howell, 1999).

Not all feminists, and not all MWMF attendees, would agree with this assessment, however. In what is perhaps the most blatant example of transphobia within feminist discourse, Janice Raymond's *The Transsexual Empire*, first published in 1979, compares the surgical pursuit of female genitalia by trans women to an act of rape. According to Raymond, rape is best defined as a violation of the integrity of a woman's body, and 'transsexuals rape women's bodies by reducing the real female form to an artifact, appropriating this body for themselves' (Raymond, 2006, p.134). Predictably, Raymond is quick to extend the rape metaphor to the example of trans women who identify as lesbian-feminists. Raymond believes that a trans woman who identifies as a lesbian-feminist 'feeds off woman's true energy source, i.e., her woman-identified self'. Of the lesbian-feminist trans woman, Raymond claims, 'It is he [sic] who recognizes that if female spirit, mind, creativity, and sexuality exist anywhere in a powerful way, it is here, among lesbian-feminists' (Raymond, 2006, p.136). Raymond's version of radical feminism advances a biologically deterministic definition of what it means to be a woman, and then rejects trans women for failing to embody this definition.

Not all feminists accept the essentialism associated with radical feminism. In fact, some who are strongly opposed to biological essentialism accuse trans people of reinforcing the binary system of sex and gender. Consider, for example, that while many trans activists advocated for the inclusion of gender identity disorder (GID) as a psychological disorder in the 1980 update of the *Diagnostic and Statistical Manual of Mental Disorders* (DSM-III), many feminists repudiate GID for attempting to establish meaningful distinctions between appropriate and inappropriate forms of gender expression. It is worth noting that although many trans activists favour the continued use of GID as a medical diagnosis, the many who do not are working diligently in an effort to have it removed from the next updated edition of the DSM. Additionally, trans people who favour the continued inclusion of GID in the DSM often do so for pragmatic reasons, such as easier access to prescribed treatments, primarily hormone therapy and sex reassignment surgery. Feminists who do not identify as trans are often slow to recognize the significance of such practical considerations, and comparatively quick to express objections based on principle. What all of this reveals is that both essentialist and anti-essentialist versions of feminism have been used to justify negative attitudes toward and feelings about trans women.

Butch Women and Trans Men

The MWMF controversy deals primarily with the status of male-to-female (MTF) trans identities, but female-to-male (FTM) trans identities are far from uncomplicated.[7] Indeed, both butch women and FTM trans men[8] have been criticized in the name of feminism. For example, Sheila Jeffreys refers to sex reassignment as a 'mutilating surgery' (2003, p.1) and regards the practice of packing[9] as evidence that 'the worship of masculinity had triumphed over the lesbian feminist project of ending gender hierarchy' (2003, p.1). As Judith Halberstam[10] notes, 'Some lesbians seem to see FTMs as traitors to a "women's" movement who cross over and become the enemy' (Halberstam, 1998, p.287).

Halberstam describes an ongoing border war over the boundary between butch and trans identities, suggesting that 'lesbians have tended to erase FTMs by claiming transsexual males as lesbians who lack access to a liberating lesbian discourse' (Halberstam, 1998, p.293). An example of this tendency can be found among those who characterize Billy Tipton, not as a trans man, but rather as a lesbian trapped in a social and professional world in which there was no room for lesbian women:

> So, for example, Billy Tipton, the jazz musician who lived his life as a man and who married a woman, is often represented within lesbian history as a lesbian woman forced to hide her gender in order to advance within her profession, rather than as a transsexual man living within his chosen gender identity.
>
> (Halberstam, 1998, p.293)

In another example of the tendency to claim lesbian status for those who might just as easily be identified as trans men, Leslie Feinberg's novel *Stone Butch Blues* is usually characterized as a lesbian novel, even though it makes just as much sense to interpret the protagonist, Jess, as a trans man. This also occurs in connection with Radcliffe Hall's *The Well of Loneliness*. Like Feinberg's Jess, Hall's Stephen has always felt more like a boy than a girl, and eventually comes to present publicly as a man in at least some contexts. Even so, *The Well of Loneliness*, like *Stone Butch Blues*, is usually described not as a novel about trans identity but rather as a novel about lesbian identity.

Halberstam does not simply suggest that these examples be reinterpreted as examples of trans identities. Instead, Halberstam questions the usefulness of attempting to demarcate between butch and trans masculinities. Halberstam also questions the usefulness of the 'masculine continuum', which makes the questionable assumption that less masculine women are less likely to identify as trans men or to seek surgical or hormonal intervention, while those who are more masculine are more likely to do so. Biddy Martin identifies a wide range of problems with the notion of such a continuum:

> While the political purpose of such a continuum seems clear and compelling, namely, to challenge the stigma attached to transsexualism, and while it is true that butch lesbians have been associated historically with gender dysphoria or dysfunction, I would suggest that making gender dysphoria or gender dysfunction too central to butchness constructs butchness in negativity, curiously makes anatomy the ground of identity, and suggests that femmes, by contrast to butches, are at least implicitly gender-conformist. It also seems problematic to put gender identities, sexual object choice, gender dysphoria, transgenderism, and transsexualism on a continuum. In keeping with the effort to separate gender and sexuality in order to expose their complex imbrications and configurations with one another, it seems productive as well to consider that the categories of experience listed above are also discrete, and that our compulsion to create coherence or political solidarities suppresses the disjunctions.
>
> (Martin, 1994, p.117)

Like Halberstam, C. Jacob Hale addresses the border war over the boundary between butch and trans identities. Hale describes the manner in which the murdered body of Brandon Teena, aka Teena Brandon, has served as one of the battlefields upon which much of this border war has been fought. In a well known case popularized by Hilary Swank's stellar portrayal in the film *Boys Don't Cry* (Peirce, 1999), Brandon Teena was designated as female at birth and raised as a girl, but eventually began to enact a sufficiently masculine gender identity to be presumed male by most people. When this secret was discovered, however, Brandon Teena was raped and then murdered, presumably as punishment for violating cultural norms associated with gender, sex, and sexuality.

As Hale notes, attempts to classify Brandon Teena as butch rather than trans or as trans rather than butch are problematic, not merely because Brandon Teena is no longer available to comment on the internal experience of any alleged butch or trans subjectivity, but also because the assumption that butch and trans identities are separated by a precise boundary is itself flawed:

> When the border wars are virophagic, eating the flesh of the living, we might better be able to access relevant information about the lives of those whom we would place on the butch or the ftm side of the

divide. Even if we have such information and can be confident that it is reliable, there are still serious problems with definitions here. The most likely clusters of characteristics to invoke definitionally are those of masculine subjectivity and the accessing of medically regulated technologies for male reembodiment.

(Hale, 1998, p.321)

Hale goes on to explore the use of these features – namely the experience of masculine subjectivity and the medical pursuit of masculine embodiment – to differentiate between butch and trans. Hale notes, first, that both butch women and trans men experience masculine subjectivity and, second, that not all trans men pursue or intend to pursue medical intervention.

Things are not any clearer with regard to trans women than they are with trans men. Not all feminine men identify as trans women, nor do all who identify as trans women pursue surgery or use hormones. There is also the additional phenomenon of drag, which further complicates the distinction between both butch women and trans men, as well as the distinction between feminine men and trans women. Drag involves the temporary participation, usually as part of a stage performance, in a highly exaggerated expression of a gender category which is often but not always different from the gender category one normally occupies. Cross-dressing involves wearing clothing and accessories associated with a gender category one does not normally occupy, sometimes in connection with sexual arousal or satisfaction. Although drag and cross-dressing are often conceptualized as existing somewhere along a continuum between conventional identities and trans identities, some drag performers and some cross-dressers conform to cultural expectations about gender, sex, and sexuality in virtually every other way. In other words, some drag performers and some cross-dressers enact their day-to-day identities as women and men in ways that are utterly unremarkable.

All of this supports Halberstam's twofold suggestion, first, that the boundary separating butch women and trans men is subject to ongoing negotiation and, second, that there is not even a continuum that draws a straight line from butch to trans. Instead, it seems that the various identity categories that are generally believed to be at least loosely related to trans identities are socially constructed and constantly negotiated.

Queer Theory

Sandy Stone offers a way of thinking about women and men, particularly trans women and trans men, that queers the existing binary:

To foreground the practices of inscription and reading which are part of this deliberate invocation of dissonance, I suggest constituting transsexuals not as a class or problematic 'third gender', but rather as a genre – a set of embodied texts whose potential for productive disruption of structured sexualities and spectra of desire has yet to be explored.

(Stone, n.d.)

In other words, trans identities serve to destabilize the familiar binary categories, female and male. It is not immediately obvious, however, just how the essentialism that seems to underlie trans identity can be rendered consistent with the anti-essentialism often associated with queer theory.

As a critic of both queer theory and trans identity, Sheila Jeffreys suggests that those who simultaneously subscribe to queer theory and recognize even the abstract possibility of trans identities, let alone those who come out as trans or who advocate on behalf of trans people, thereby betray an internal conflict:

Unless we accept that there is such a thing as a real and essential transsexualism, a notion which should be antithetical to queer theory's supposed anti-essentialism, then the inclusion of this category within queer politics does seem extraordinary. It defies the proud pro-lesbian and gay politics that are required in a liberation movement by celebrating the castration of those who love the same sex. The inclusion of transsexuals also supports the notion that gender is essential, and the most retrograde notions of gender at that.

(Jeffreys, 2003, p.49)

Jeffreys' concern over the essentialism that allegedly underlies trans identities seems misplaced, given that Jeffreys subscribes to gender stereotypes that are especially insidious and irredeemably essentialist. According to Jeffreys, for example, gay men are promiscuous because they have missed out on the training in temperance and sexual restraint that heterosexual men receive through their relationships with women, presumably because women are inherently more modest about sex than men are (Jeffreys, 2003, pp.72–3). Although Jeffreys' own position is easily dismissed as mere stereotyping, this observation does not itself answer the question about the apparent conflict between queer theory and the alleged essentialism of trans identities.

In response to Jeffreys, it is possible to respect, even to celebrate, trans identities without thereby suggesting that the importance some trans people place on bodily manifestations of feminine or masculine subjectivities matters equally to all people – even to all trans people.

As Biddy Martin notes, 'the opposition set up between conventional understandings of gender as stable core and postmodern conceptions of identity as the effect of discursive practice needs to be displaced, not decided in one direction or the other' (Martin, 1994, p.118). It is important to recognize that trusting people to determine for themselves which identity categories feel the most authentic or natural is a simple matter of respecting their human dignity and rightful autonomy. This does not in any way preclude the celebration of what is sometimes referred to as *cisgender* identity, namely the gender normative identities of those who exist unproblematically as women or men.[11] Nor does it preclude the simultaneous celebration of *genderqueer* identities that expose the 'mismatches between sex, gender and sexual desire' (Jagose, 1996, p.3) for those who are unwilling or unable to define themselves in terms of the established binary.

In this context, rejecting essentialism means accepting that 'women' and 'men' are categories that have been and continue to be affected by social processes. This acceptance serves as an invitation to construct alternative categories. The construction of alternative categories, however, need not entail the wholesale rejection of the existing categories. One way to challenge a binary is to deny or ignore the distinction it draws, for example, by denying or ignoring the distinction between women and men. This approach, which Jeffreys seems to regard as the only approach possible, ignores the significance that the distinction between women and men holds for many people, including many trans people. A more inviting way to challenge the existing binary is to construct additional alternatives, so that instead of just two categories there are many. By challenging the binary in this manner, queer theory is capable of resisting essentialism while simultaneously affirming the experiences of people for whom the established categories are problematic as well as people for whom the established categories are relatively unproblematic.

Additional Resources

- Cvetkovich, A. and Wahng, S. (2001). 'Don't stop the music: Roundtable discussion with workers from the Michigan womyn's music festival'. *GLQ: A Journal of Lesbian and Gay Studies*, 7(1), 131–51.
- Serano, J. (2007). 'Trans Woman Manifesto'. In *Whipping Girl: A Transsexual Woman on Sexism and the Scapegoating of Femininity* (pp.11–20). Emeryville, CA: Seal Press 2007.
- Halberstam, J. and Hale, C. J. (1998). 'Butch/FTM border wars'. *GLQ: A Journal of Lesbian and Gay Studies*, 4(2), 283–5.
- Halberstam, J. (1998). 'Transgender butch: Butch/FTM border wars and the masculine continuum'. *GLQ: A Journal of Lesbian and Gay Studies*, 4(2), 287–310.
- Hale, C. J. (1998). 'Consuming the living, dis(re)membering the dead in the

butch/FTM Borderlands'. *GLQ: A Journal of Lesbian and Gay Studies*, 4(2), 311–48.
- Stone, S. (n.d.). *The* Empire *Strikes Back.* Available online at http://www.sandystone.com/empire-strikes-back. First published as Stone, S. (1991). In K. Straub and J. Epstein (eds), *Body Guards: The Cultural Politics of Gender Ambiguity*, New York: Routledge.
- Feinberg, L. (1993). *Stone Butch Blues.* San Francisco: Firebrand Books.
- Baur, G. (2002) *Venus Boyz.* Clockwise Productions.

References

Baum, L. F. (2005). *15 Books in 1: L. Frank Baum's Original 'Oz' Series.* Shoes and Ships and Sealing Wax, Ltd. (Original works published 1908–20).

Baur, G. (2002) *Venus Boyz.* Clockwise Productions.

BethX (1999). 'Trans exclusion at Michigan women's music festival'. *AntiJen Pages: A Young Transsexual Newsletter*, vol.1, December 1999. Retrieved 15 April 2010 from http://eminism.org/michigan/19991201-bethx.txt.

Cvetkovich, A. and Wahng, S. (2001). 'Don't stop the music: Roundtable discussion with workers from the Michigan womyn's music festival'. *GLQ: A Journal of Lesbian and Gay Studies*, 7(1), 131–51.

Feinberg, L. (1993). *Stone Butch Blues.* San Francisco: Firebrand Books.

Halberstam, J. (1998). 'Transgender butch: Butch/FTM border wars and the masculine continuum'. *GLQ: A Journal of Lesbian and Gay Studies*, 4(2), 287–310.

Halberstam, J. and Hale, C. J. (1998). 'Butch/FTM border wars'. *GLQ: A Journal of Lesbian and Gay Studies*, 4(2), 283–5.

Hale, C. J. (1998). 'Consuming the living, dis(re)membering the dead in the butch/FTM Borderlands'. *GLQ: A Journal of Lesbian and Gay Studies*, 4(2), 311–48.

Howell, C. (1999). *Protest Called For – Women's Music Festival Discriminatory Policy Still in Effect.* Press release, 24 June 1999. Retrieved 15 April 2010 from http://eminism.org/michigan/19990624-gpac.txt.

Jagose, A. (1996). *Queer Theory: An Introduction.* New York: NYU Press.

Jeffreys, S. (2003). *Unpacking Queer Politics.* Malden, MA: Polity Press.

Koyama, E. (n.d.). *Michigan/Trans Controversy Archive.* Retrieved 15 April 2010 from http://www.eminism.org/michigan.

Koyama, E. (n.d.). *Michigan/Trans Controversy FAQ: Introduction.* Retrieved 15 April 2010 from http://eminism.org/michigan/faq-intro.html.

Lamm, N., *et al.* (2001). *MWMF Trans-inclusion Petition.* Retrieved 15 April 2010 from http://eminism.org/michigan/20011218-lamm.txt.

Martin, B. (1994). 'Sexualities without genders and other queer utopias'. *Diacritics*, 24(2–3), 104–21.

Oven Productions (1975). *Why Women-only Concerts?* Statement released 1975. Retrieved 15 April 2010 from http://eminism.org/michigan/womenonly.gif.

Peirce, K. (1999). *Boys Don't Cry.* Twentieth Century Fox.

Raymond, J. (2006). 'Sappho by surgery: The transsexually constructed lesbian-feminist'. In S. Stryker and S. Whittle (eds), *The Transgender Studies Reader*, New York: Routledge (original work published 1979).

Serano, J. (2007). *Whipping Girl: A Transsexual Woman on Sexism and the Scapegoating of Femininity.* Emeryville, CA: Seal Press 2007.

Stone, S. (n.d.). *The* Empire *Strikes Back*. Retrieved 25 March 2010 from http://www.sandystone.com/empire-strikes-back. First published as Stone, S. (1991). In K. Straub and J. Epstein (eds), *Body Guards: The Cultural Politics of Gender Ambiguity*, New York: Routledge.

Vogel, L. (2000). *Michigan Womyn's Music Festival Affirms Womyn-born Space*. Press release, 24 July 2000. Retrieved 15 April 2010 from http://eminism.org/michigan/20000724-vogel.txt.

Notes

1   'Womyn' is sometimes used instead of 'wo*men*' and 'womon' is used instead of 'wo*man*' as an alternative to the use of terminology that is referential of men and masculinity.

2   Various forms of feminism, including radical feminism, are discussed in some detail in Chapter 7.

3   For further background and discussion of the MWMF controversy, refer to the collection of articles and links archived by Emi Koyama at http://www.eminism.org/michigan.

4   The concept of gender is discussed in some detail in Chapter 6.

5   There are many exceptions to this generalization. Serano's *Whipping Girl* (2007), for example, refers not to transgender identity, but to transsexual identity, in its intersecting analysis of feminist and trans identity.

6   For further information about Camp Trans, refer to http://www.camp-trans.org.

7   The abbreviation MTF is sometimes used to make quick and easy reference to male-to-female transgender people, or trans women, and the abbreviation FTM is sometimes used to make quick and easy reference to female-to-male transgender people, or trans men.

8   Butch is often used in reference to some women, including some lesbian women, who exhibit a traditionally masculine personal style without identifying as male. In other words, butch women (or simply, butches) do not identify as transgender. Butch identity is sometimes contrasted with the traditionally feminine style of femme women (or simply, femmes).

9   In this context, packing refers to the practice among some trans men, and even some butch women, of wearing a dildo or other prosthetic under the clothing in order to approximate the bodily presence of a penis.

10 Although the works cited here were published as Judith, Halberstam has recently begun self-identifying as Judith/Jack Halberstam, Judith 'Jack' Halberstam, or soemtimes just 'Jack' Halberstam.

11 The term cisgender was introduced as a way to refer to those who are not transgender without resorting to words like 'biological' or 'regular', which inevitably imply that the gender expression of people who do not identify as transgender is more authentic than or otherwise preferable to the gender expression of people who do identify as transgender. According to some people, however, cisgender is a problematic, perhaps even self-defeating, term because it can be interpreted as suggesting that those who identify as lesbian, gay, or bisexual, for example, but not as transgender, experience no mismatch between their own gender identity and gender expression and cultural expectations regarding gender identity and expression.

SECTION III

GENDER

The girl was getting used to queer adventures,
which interested her very much.

(L. Frank Baum, *The Road to Oz*, p.167)

6

Gender Defined and Undefined

In spite of this queer make-up, the Patchwork Girl was magically alive and had proved herself not the least jolly and agreeable of the many quaint characters who inhabit the astonishing Fairyland of Oz.

(L. Frank Baum, *The Lost Princess of Oz*, p.454)

The Sex-Gender Distinction

Dominant group identities form by way of a contrast between members of a particular identity category and everyone else. It makes sense to categorize some people as women only in virtue of the distinction between women and men. It likewise makes sense to categorize some people as lesbian or gay only in virtue of the distinction between homosexuality and heterosexuality. The dominant group is defined by whom it excludes, and not merely by whom it includes. The identification of someone or something as different from oneself is often referred to as *alterity*. In the 1949 feminist classic, *The Second Sex*, philosopher Simone de Beauvoir suggested that virtually any group of people – regardless of what binds its various members – will eventually come to regard all others as outsiders.

> Thus it is that no group ever sets itself up as the One without at once setting up the Other over against itself. If three travelers chance to occupy the same compartment, that is enough to make vaguely hostile 'others' out of all the rest of the passengers on the train. In small-town eyes all persons not belonging to the village are 'strangers' and suspect; to the native of a country all who inhabit other countries are 'foreigners'; Jews are 'different' for the anti-Semite, Negroes are 'inferior' for American racists, aborigines are 'natives' for colonists, proletarians are the 'lower class' for the privileged.
>
> (Beauvoir, 1974, pp.xix–xx)

There is no shortage of examples of this phenomenon. For example, people from the same home town often share a kindred bond in virtue of their common experience, and a similar bond can be found among those who appreciate the same art, music, sport, or hobby. It should come as no surprise, then, that the distinction between boys and girls in early childhood sometimes leads, in older children and adults, to a sense of solidarity among those who identify as 'real' men or 'real' women – and an attempt to assimilate by many who do not.

Although Beauvoir seemed critical of this tendency, especially when manifested in the form of sexism, a commitment to what could be described as the inevitability of alterity does not invite optimism about avoiding the inequalities that often result from the distinction between insiders and outsiders; between 'us' and 'them'. Beauvoir was not alone in suggesting that the tendency to make such distinctions is characteristic of the human condition. Many, particularly those who are reluctant to disrupt existing hierarchies, use this point to defend their resistance to social change. Consider, for instance, those who reject feminism on the assumption that it favours women over men, or those who oppose affirmative action programmes on the assumption that they favour minority groups over the dominant group. Lurking beneath these assumptions is the notion that established distinctions, such as those based on sex and race, are lasting divisions that would endure even major shifts in the existing power structure.[1] According to this line of reasoning, as long as there are differences, for example, between male and female reproductive organs, we will continue to divide ourselves in virtue of such differences.

A more complicated version of Beauvoir's point is present in the suggestion that feminism, as a form of identity politics,[2] will inevitably fail because the identity categories, such as sex and gender, that promise to unite a group of people are always mitigated by additional categories that ultimately divide the members of that group. On this view, the differences that separate women from men are insufficient to unify women against sexism given the additional differences that separate women on the basis of racial identity, ethnic identity, class identity, sexual identity, and so on. This carries Beauvoir's reasoning to its logical extreme, suggesting that after separating themselves from passengers in the other compartments, the travellers would soon subdivide into those on the left side of the train and those on the right, those by the window and those by the aisle, until none of them could experience solidarity with any other. Although there does seem to be a tendency for people to differentiate between 'us' and 'them', it does not necessarily follow that oppression is an inherent or necessary function of identifying someone or something as different, or 'other'. Beauvoir would likely agree that there is a qualitative difference between the distinction drawn between 'us' and 'them' by people who happen to be travelling together and the distinction between 'us' and 'them' drawn on the basis of such presumably fixed categories as sex or race.

As an existentialist, Beauvoir was concerned about the tension between freedom and determinism and believed that there is nothing necessary or inevitable about who a person ultimately becomes.[3] Applied to the distinction between women and men, this means that one must become a woman in order to be a woman. The process of becoming a woman is intimately intertwined with the process by which someone is identified as or differentiated from a man. The male self is asserted as the subject, or the 'One' only by identifying the female as the object, or the 'Other.' As Marilyn Frye explains:

> So he conjures an object that is object but not also subject, which he can oppose but which will not oppose him – which does not require a reciprocal relation. Not a 'relative' other (who is also subject and demands reciprocity), but an 'absolute' Other. This subject is male/ masculine, which Beauvoir both acknowledges and accepts when she says that woman is the Other – the 'absolute Other' posed by the (male) subject. It is through posing the Other – woman – that the subject constructs himself... as One and sovereign, secure and safe. Becoming a woman is becoming an 'absolute' Other. One cannot be a woman and be a subject.
>
> (Frye, 1996, p.993)

This explanation of how people come to identify as women and men suggests that these identity categories are contingent. To regard them as contingent is to acknowledge that they could have been, and perhaps could yet be, other than they are. By recognizing that 'no subset of human beings is destined by biology or a distinctive essence to being the absolute Other' (Frye, 1996, p.994), Beauvoir anticipated what would eventually be identified as the sex-gender distinction.

In the 1970s, some feminist scholars began using 'gender', a term borrowed from linguistics, to distinguish socially learned differences between women and men from biologically innate differences.[4] It seems obvious to many people that clothing styles and grooming habits are social, for example, while genital structures are biological.[5] There is no clear consensus regarding some of the many characteristics associated with the distinction between women and men, however. Whether there is a biological basis for the twofold characterization of men as more aggressive than women and women as more nurturing than men is open to debate, even among feminists.[6] The mere recognition that there is a distinction between sex and gender does not reveal which differences are sex differences and which are gender differences. In other words, the distinction between sex and gender does not itself determine which of the characteristics commonly associated with women belong to the female sex and which belong instead to the feminine gender, and it does not determine which of the characteristics commonly associated with men belong to the male sex and which belong instead to the masculine gender.

A potential source of confusion regarding the concept of gender is the fact that, in addition to referring to socially learned differences between women and men, gender is also used in at least two additional ways. In a second and closely related usage, gender refers to the mind, while sex refers to the body. Used in this manner, gender refers to private mental experiences, such as the experience of feeling 'like a woman' or feeling 'like a man' that can occur independent of biological sex. In a third and potentially more problematic usage, gender is used virtually interchangeably with sex in reference to any of the characteristics by which women and men can be differentiated.

Another source of confusion in connection with the distinction between sex and gender derives from the recognition that the physical characteristics, both of whole populations and of particular members, all have unique social histories. The boundary between that which is social and that which is biological is not nearly as crisp as implied by some feminist discussions. Consider, for instance, that all of the different dog breeds in existence today are the deliberate result of an ongoing[7] process of selective breeding,[8] and yet they are also biologically distinct enough for individual dogs to be judged in shows as better or worse examples of different breeds. That all dogs from poodles to pitbulls came about through social processes does not mean that specific poodles and pitbulls do not now exist in reality, nor does it mean that the differences among various instantiations of different breeds can be imagined away. This example debunks the hasty assumption that social phenomena and biological phenomena are mutually exclusive, and it demonstrates the very real impact of social phenomena on physical bodies.

In another example of social processes impacting physical bodies, recent research (Cochran and Harpending, 2009) indicates that the ability to digest milk beyond infancy developed only within the past 10,000 years, only in some cultures, and only in connection with the domestication of certain livestock, including camels and cattle. One explanation is that the ability to consume dairy products offered greater survival potential, particularly during times of famine, and those with a genetic mutation that allowed for uninterrupted production of lactose, the enzyme that digests milk sugar, had an evolutionary advantage. In contemporary western parlance, the expression 'lactose intolerance' marks the inability to process dairy products as an aberration. In fact, the aberration occurred when various cultures stopped outgrowing the lactose tolerance necessary for nursing during infancy. In a related example, a wealth of empirical research (Lewis, 1975; Pande, 2003; Mishra, *et al.*, 2004; and Spruijt-Metz, *et al.*, 2006) suggests that there are significant disparities around the world in the treatment of female and male infants, including disparities in feeding and nutrition. It seems possible that the tendency to encourage infant boys to nurse longer and eat more than infant girls may be at least partially responsible for some of the physical differences between adult women and men, particularly differences linked to early childhood nutrition, such as height and weight. In addition to demonstrating the wisdom that underlies the old adage, 'You are what you eat', these examples also reveal that even biological characteristics reflect the environmental context in which they are situated. This does not amount merely to the attractive but relatively trite notion that nature and nurture both shape human development, but rather to the somewhat more subtle suggestion that bodies are themselves moulded by the social environment from which they emerge.

Gender-Neutral and Gender-Inclusive Language

The obscured boundary between nature and nurture notwithstanding, the distinction between sex and gender is nevertheless a useful heuristic[9] for acknowledging the extent to which current ideas and ideals about women and men are culturally contingent. The distinction between sex and gender provides a conceptual framework for recognizing the existence of some differences between women and men, including some biological differences, without thereby assuming that all differences are biological. It also issues an invitation to engage in a critical examination of various aspects of the social environment and to explore the possibility of changing that environment to avoid the perpetuation of existing gender roles. In a particularly poignant example of such exploration, Marge Piercy's feminist science fiction classic, *Woman on the Edge of Time*, imagines a utopian society, Mattapoisett, that is free of gender socialization and gender roles (Piercy, 1976). In the utopian future world of Mattapoisett, the life histories and, as a result, the bodies of women and men are virtually indistinguishable. In Piercy's Mattapoisett, 'person' replaces the nominative case gender pronouns 'she' and 'he', while 'per' replaces the possessive and objective case pronouns 'her', 'his', and 'him.'

Despite the allegedly neutral use of 'man', 'he', 'his', and 'him' to refer in the abstract to any generic person, these terms inevitably seem to grant priority to men and masculinity.[10] Granting linguistic priority to any one social group sends a powerful message about who matters and who does not. For this reason, people, both individually and collectively, struggled and continue to struggle to articulate better and worse ways of addressing the issue of gender in language. Consider, for example, the guidelines accepted in 1986 by the American Philosophical Association on the 'nonsexist use of language' within philosophy (Warren, 1986), the 1991 statement by the American Psychological Association on avoiding 'heterosexual bias', or Jacob Hale's more recent articulation of a set of rules 'for non-transsexuals

writing about transsexuals, transsexuality, transsexualism, or trans ___'.
Consider also the campaign to replace 'she' and 'he' with 'ze', and to
replace 'her', 'his', and 'him' with 'hir'. This strategy enjoyed some limited
and localized successes in the 1970s, and is preferred even today by some
people, including some transgender and intersex people, who do not fit
straightforwardly or unproblematically into exactly one gender category,
female or male. Leslie Feinberg, for example, who was categorized as
biologically female upon birth, eventually developed a more masculine
identity, and now prefers to be referred to by the pronouns 'ze', 'hir',
and 'hirself'.[11] Although these were initially intended as gender-neutral
replacement terms for 'she', 'he', 'her', 'his', and 'him', they are now used,
if they are used at all, not instead of, but in addition to more familiar
gender-specific pronouns. 'She' and 'her' are still used for those who are
unquestionably female; 'he', 'him', and 'his' are still used for those who are
unquestionably male; and 'ze' and 'hir' are rarely used, except in reference
to those who resist binary classification.

Alternative gender pronouns, like 'ze' and 'hir', can be used in addition
to or instead of the more familiar gender pronouns, 'she', 'he', 'her',
'him', and 'his.' This emphasizes an important difference between the
use of gender-neutral and gender-inclusive language. Language is neutral
when a single term is used to refer equally to all of the different categories
of people. Language is inclusive when multiple terms are used to refer
separately and specifically to more than one, and ideally to all, relevant
categories of people. Gender neutrality and gender inclusivity are two
different ways of addressing the symbolic priority that has been granted
to men and masculinity in recent history. The wholesale replacement of
'he' and 'she' with 'ze', and of 'her' and 'his' with 'hir', would mark a
transition from gender-specific language to gender-neutral language. The
addition of 'ze' and 'hir' as third options in cases where 'she' and 'he' or
'her' and 'his' do not fit, however, is a transition, not to gender-neutral
language, but rather to gender-inclusive, or at least more gender-inclusive
language. While the simultaneous use of both 'he' and 'she' acknowledges
a range of gender possibilities that is more inclusive than just 'he', the
simultaneous use of 'he', 'she', and 'ze' acknowledges a range of gender
possibilities that is even more inclusive.

Despite limited use by Leslie Feinberg and a few other noteworthy
examples, the attempted introduction of new gender pronouns was
largely unsuccessful. Even so, there have been some gradual and lasting
changes in response to feminist concerns about linguistic bias. Consider,
for example, the now familiar use of 'he or she', 'he/she', '(s)he', or even
'they'[12] to refer to a generic or hypothetical person. Compare this with
the recent past, when US schoolchildren were taught that it was necessary
to use 'he' and 'his' when referring to a person in the abstract. Also
consider the fairly recent transition from using such gender-specific terms
as 'waiter', 'waitress', 'salesman', 'stewardess', and the like, to using

gender-neutral terms such as 'server', 'salesperson', 'flight attendant', and so on. Consider, finally, the growing tendency to substitute 'people' or 'humankind' for 'man' and 'mankind'.

In some contexts, the implementation of gender-neutral language has been more successful than the implementation of gender-inclusive language, and in other contexts the implementation of gender-inclusive language has been more successful. In many, perhaps even most, contexts related to employment, gender-neutral terminology currently prevails. In some cases, this transition to gender-neutral language has been achieved through the elimination of terms that were once used to signal female or feminine identity, as in the growing tendency to replace 'actress' with 'actor' in reference to both male and female performers. In other cases, new terminology has been introduced to replace gender-specific terminology of the past, as with the growing tendency to replace 'mailman', 'fireman', and the like with terms such as 'letter carrier', 'firefighter', and so forth. Through the simple elimination of terms marked as feminine, and through the introduction of entirely new terms, many job titles have been revised to avoid any reference to the sex or gender of the worker. Once commonplace, it now seems vaguely offensive to draw attention to sex and gender with expressions such as 'male nurse' and 'female cop', which imply that it is unexpected and therefore worthy of comment for a man to become a nurse or for a woman to become a police officer.

In other contexts, however, the trend seems to favour gender-inclusive terminology over gender-neutral terminology. One example is the widespread use of both 'gay' and 'lesbian', rather than just 'gay', to refer to women and men whose primary erotic orientation is towards members of the same sex. Just as 'man' can be used generically to refer to women and men, 'gay' can also be used generically to refer to women and men who identify as homosexual. But just as the gender-specific meaning of 'man' can interfere with its intended gender-neutral meaning, the gender-specific meaning of 'gay' can also interfere with its intended gender-neutral meaning. Even if they mean to refer to women and men alike, statements like, 'The *man* selected for the new management position will receive a substantial raise in pay', or 'Any employee who would like to be considered for promotion must submit *his* resumé by Friday', may inadvertently imply that women will not be given serious consideration. Similarly, a statement such as 'We are committed to addressing a range of *gay* issues' carries the subtle suggestion that the primary concern will be issues that confront gay men, and not necessarily those that confront lesbian women. Even ostensibly neutral terms, like 'person' instead of 'man', or 'homosexual' instead of 'gay', may be insufficient to signal the intent to include women. If all previous management positions have been filled by men, simply switching from 'man' to 'person' will not necessarily convey the intention to give equal consideration to women this time around.

Gender-inclusive language avoids this sort of ambiguity by making direct and explicit reference to women. By making direct and explicit reference to women, gender-inclusive language also implies that there are relevant and significant differences between women and men in the given context. Reference not just to gay issues, but to gay and lesbian issues, implies that what matters most to lesbian women may be of less interest to gay men, and vice versa. In the context of health care, for example, lesbian women as a group may have more interest in breast cancer prevention and treatment, while gay men as a group may have more interest in HIV/AIDS prevention and treatment. Gender-neutral terms refer interchangeably to members of all sex and gender categories, thereby suggesting that women, men, and everyone else, are semantically equivalent. In some cases, then, the transition from neutral terms, like 'one' and 'people', to more inclusive terms, like 'he or she' and 'women and men', constitutes a rejection of the assumption that women and men are fundamentally the same.

Unlike gender-neutral language, gender-inclusive language specifies all categories intended for recognition. Because it specifies all categories intended for recognition, however, allegedly inclusive language inevitably excludes those to whom no direct reference is made. References to both women and men may be more inclusive than references just to men but, unlike references to people in general, references to women and men inadvertently exclude people to whom the binary categories of sex and gender do not readily apply, notably transgender and intersex people. By the same token, references to both lesbian women and gay men may be more inclusive than references to just gay men but, unlike references to people in general, references to lesbian women and gay men once again exclude people to whom the binary categories of sexuality do not readily apply, notably those who identify as bisexual, polyamorous, asexual, or otherwise outside the dichotomy between homosexual and heterosexual orientation.

The distinction between inclusivity and neutrality in connection with the discourse surrounding gender, sex, and sexuality also has a counterpart in connection with the discourse surrounding race and ethnicity. Just as allegedly neutral terms like 'people' and 'humankind' have been, and often are still, associated with members of the dominant categories of gender, sex, and sexuality, they also have been, and often are still, associated with members of the dominant racial and ethnic categories. In principle, gender-neutral terms, such as 'person' or 'people' refer equally and literally to all people, including transgender and intersex people. In practice, unfortunately, the priority in contemporary US and European culture granted to men (Moulton, 1977), more specifically to heterosexual men, and even more specifically to white, European or north-American, formally educated, upper-middle class, able-bodied, Christian, heterosexual men, is so deeply entrenched that what comes to mind as the generic person, quite often, is a white, European or north-American, formally educated, upper-middle class, able-bodied, Christian, heterosexual man.[13]

The Hegemonic Binary

Gender-neutral and gender-inclusive language, or rather, attempted gender-neutral and gender-inclusive language, is inadvertently but inevitably exclusionary. What interferes with neutrality is the priority implicitly granted to members of historically privileged categories, such as heterosexual men. What interferes with inclusivity is the priority explicitly granted to members of the categories targeted for inclusion, such as women and men, or even lesbian women and gay men. Allegedly gender-inclusive language ultimately reinforces a familiar division of the human world into two basic categories. Whether the division is between female and male, feminine and masculine, women and men, lesbian women and gay men, or whatever, is largely irrelevant. It is irrelevant because the binary system of gender, sex, and sexuality is not just an unrelated set of categories, some involving biological sex and others involving learned behaviours and social or sexual roles. Rather, it is a holistic framework that regards gender, sex, and sexuality as expressions of a basic division of the human world into two distinct *natural kinds*.

The traditional doctrine of natural kinds reflects an underlying commitment to essentialism about the natural world.[14] According to John Dupré (1993), there are three conditions that must be met according to essentialist versions of the doctrine of natural kinds: first, natural kind categories should be clearly and unambiguously delineated. Second, natural kind categories should be a product of discovery rather than invention or creation. Third, natural kind categories should reveal as much information as possible about the members of those categories – and, ideally, they will reveal *all* of the essential characteristics of those members (Dupré, 1993, pp.17–18). The traditional, essentialist, doctrine of natural kinds depicts an orderly world that divides into thoroughly informative categories inclusive of all phenomena without leftovers or crossovers.[15]

Hilary Kornblith represents natural kinds as 'homeostatic property clusters' in which underlying structures produce the observable properties that are distinctive of various natural kinds (Kornblith, 1993). Kornblith suggests that experience reveals which properties and which sorts of properties are indicative of relevant underlying structural differences. Although Kornblith does not make direct reference to the properties associated with gender, sex, and sexuality, these properties are commonly believed to form clusters around the two natural kinds into which the human world divides. One of these two presumed natural kinds includes people who are anatomically male and characteristically masculine with a dominant sexuality that is oriented toward others who are anatomically female and characteristically feminine with a submissive sexuality that is, in turn, oriented toward those who are anatomically male and characteristically masculine. The other includes people who are anatomically female and characteristically feminine with a submissive sexuality that is oriented toward others who are anatomically male and characteristically masculine with a dominant sexuality that is, in turn, oriented toward those who are anatomically female and characteristically feminine. These two categories comprise what is usefully described as the *hegemonic binary*.[16] In service of a deeply essentialist account of gender, sex, and sexuality, the hegemonic binary refers to the coalescence of gender, sex, and sexuality into exactly two fundamentally distinct natural kinds: women and men (refer to Figure 6.1).

Figure 6.1 The hegemonic binary

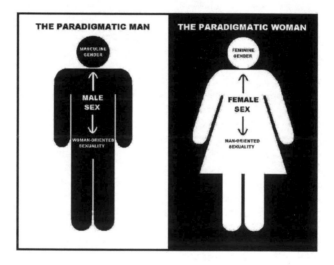

The concept of natural kinds does not assume that all individuals will exemplify their respective categories equally well. What it does assume, however, is that those who do not exemplify the categories to which they belong are best understood as defective. Consider, for example, the features commonly assumed to be definitive of human beings. There are many, many different features associated with this category, which is widely regarded as a natural kind category. Prominent examples include the relatively high-level cognitive functioning and the upright bodily posture that are widely believed to differentiate *homo sapiens* from other primates. For this reason, people who are not in full possession of these features are commonly regarded as disabled or even, at worst, as defective or deformed. Natural kinds do not just organize the natural and social world; they also provide a basis for evaluating and ranking various individuals according to how closely they conform to the ideal.

In this respect, the concept of natural kinds functions much like the concept of Platonic Forms.[17] The theory of the Forms is addressed in many of Plato's works, but the allegory of the prisoners in the cave in Book VII of the *The Republic* offers a particularly vivid exposition (Plato, 1991, pp.253–61). The allegory of the cave describes a group of prisoners chained up in such a way that they can see only shadows on the cave wall in front of them. The shadows are produced by physical objects placed before the fire behind them. An analogy is drawn between these imperfect shadows and the imperfection of the physical world. Just as physical objects are more real and more perfect than mere shadows, so too are the Forms more real and more perfect than any of the particular things encountered in the everyday world. Unlike the particulars that populate the everyday world, Forms are perfect, eternal, universal abstractions, much like the concepts or categories of which the various particular things are members.

If women and men constitute natural kinds, and natural kinds function as Platonic Forms, then it is no surprise that people approximate, but do not fully instantiate, the categories they represent. Just as the ancient ideal of masculine perfection represented in the figure of Adonis was not realized by the average Greek citizen, the average member of contemporary western culture is a similarly flawed representative of the idealized category of womanhood or manhood. It is important to recognize that people who deviate from the characteristics that are believed to define the categories to which they belong are not usually regarded as evidence against those defining characteristics. Instead, and conveniently, those defining characteristics are usually used as evidence that there is something wrong with the people in question. Those who do not manifest what Judith Butler (1990) refers to as 'intelligible' genders are regarded, at best, as different and, at worst, as deviant. According to Butler, genders are 'intelligible' to the extent that they 'in some sense institute and maintain relations of coherence and continuity among sex, gender, sexual practice, and desire' (Butler, 1990, p.17). In other words, genders are 'intelligible' to the extent that they reflect and reinforce the hegemonic binary.

It is also important to recognize that the distinction between women and men is not just a straightforward division between two separate but equal categories, natural kinds, or Platonic Forms. Implicit in the distinction between women and men is an understanding of man as the ideal. In fact, the distinction between the perfect Form and the imperfect copy is replicated in the distinction between woman and man, female and male, feminine and masculine. That which is characteristically female or feminine is generally regarded as inferior to that which is characteristically male or masculine. As a result, women are in a contradictory situation such that meeting cultural expectations regarding ideal femininity would automatically mean failing to meet cultural expectations regarding the human ideal, and meeting cultural expectations regarding the human ideal would mean failing to meet cultural expectations of ideal femininity.

To conceptualize 'women' and 'men' as natural kind categories is to accept the twofold belief, first, that women and men are quite different from one another and, second, that the fundamental differences between women and men are attributable primarily to biology. In addition to referring to biological kinds, however, 'women' and 'men' are sometimes understood to refer to what biologically male and female human beings become as the result of gender socialization. According to this second usage, 'women' and 'men' are not natural kind categories, but rather, they are categories that exist at the intersection of nature and nurture. In yet a third usage, 'women' and 'men' are regarded as purely social or experiential categories. To put it another way, the terms 'women' and 'men' sometimes designate sex, they sometimes designate gender, and they sometimes designate the product of both sex and gender. It makes as much sense, for example, to make the ostensibly biological claim that 'Women produce eggs' as it does to make the more obviously social claim that 'Men enjoy football'.

The ability to transition seamlessly from a biological conception of 'gender' to a social one, or from biological definitions of 'women' and 'men' to social ones, reinforces the hegemonic binary, which regards gender and sex, and even sexuality, as different expressions of the same fundamental division of the human world into its most basic natural kinds.[18] Judith Lorber provides an apt description of the processes that shape gender, sex, and sexuality.

> For the individual, gender construction starts with assignment to a sex category on the basis of what the genitalia look like at birth. Then babies are dressed or adorned in a way that displays the category because parents don't want to be constantly asked whether their baby is a girl or a boy. A sex category becomes a gender status through naming, dress, and the use of other gender markers. Once a child's gender is evident, others treat those in one gender differently from those in the other, and the children respond to the different treatment by feeling different and behaving differently. As soon as they can talk, they start to refer to themselves as members of their gender. Sex doesn't come into play again until puberty, but by that time, sexual feelings and desires and practices have been shaped by gendered norms and expectations.
>
> (Lorber, 1994, p.14)

Following a trend associated with Judith Butler, Lorber refers to gender as an action or a process, rather than a static state or condition. Understood in this manner, gender is not so much who people are but what they do. Indeed, Lorber suggests that 'everyone "does gender" without thinking about it' (Lorber, 1994, p.13). Borrowing from the example of drag performance, Butler indicates that, unlike the imitation of the Forms, the imitation that occurs in drag, or any other performance of gender, is an imitation that has no original. There is not something real that gender imitates. What gender imitates is simply other performances of gender, which are themselves mere imitations. Butler remarks that '*gender is a kind of imitation for which there is no original*; in fact, it is a kind of imitation that produces the very notion of the original as an effect and consequence of the imitation itself' (Butler, 1993, p.313).

What Butler's notion of performative gender offers is, first, a recognition of the active role that everyone plays in maintaining the hegemonic binary and, second, an invitation to disrupt the hegemonic binary whenever it proves to be too constricting. Thus, instead of attempting to repair the language and meaning surrounding existing categories of gender, sex, and sexuality, there is also the option, as expressed in the title of Butler's 1990 book, of making 'Gender Trouble'. Making gender trouble simply means directing attention toward rather than away from the limitations of existing categories, particularly the existing categories of gender, sex, and sexuality associated with the hegemonic binary. Thus, rather than attempting to resolve the dispute regarding gender-neutral language and gender-inclusive language, a meaningful third option is to use the problematic existing terminology, particularly when doing so is most likely to emphasize mismatches within the categories of gender, sex, and sexuality associated with the hegemonic binary. This can also be characterized as a 'queering' of the established binaries. As explained by Anamarie Jagose, 'queer' refers to 'those gestures or analytical models which dramatize incoherencies in the allegedly stable relations between chromosomal sex, gender and sexual desire' (Jagose, 1996, p.3). To disrupt the hegemonic binary, perhaps even in very small ways, serves to 'queer' the paradigm. Making 'Gender Trouble', rather than attempting to resolve or eliminate such trouble, is thus a viable alternative for dealing with the existence of the sorts of incoherencies that Jagose seems to have in mind.

Additional Resources

- Warren, V. L. (1986). American Philosophical Association, Committee on the Status of Women in the Profession, 'Guidelines for the nonsexist use of language'. *Proceedings and Addresses of the American Philosophical Association, 59*(3), 471–84.
- American Psychological Association, Committee on Lesbian and Gay Concerns

(1991). 'Avoiding heterosexual bias in language'. *American Psychologist*, 46(9), 973–4.

- Hale, J. (n.d.). Suggested rules for non-transsexuals writing about transsexuals, transsexuality, transsexualism, or trans ___ (http://www.sandystone.com/hale. rules.html).
- Moulton, Janice (1977). 'The myth of the neutral "man"'. In M. Vetterling-Braggin, F. A. Elliston, and J. English (eds), *Feminism and Philosophy* (pp.124–37). Totowa, NJ: Littlefield Adams.
- Lorber, J. (1994). 'Night to his day: The social construction of gender'. In *Paradoxes of Gender* (pp.13–36). New Haven: Yale University Press.
- Butler, J. (1993). 'Imitation and gender insubordination'. In H. Abelove, M. A. Barale, and D. M. Halperin (eds), *The Lesbian and Gay Studies Reader* (pp.307–20). New York: Routledge.
- Piercy, M. (1976). *Woman on the Edge of Time*. New York: Alfred A. Knopf.

References

American Psychological Association, Committee on Lesbian and Gay Concerns (1991). 'Avoiding heterosexual bias in language'. *American Psychologist*, 46(9), 973–4.

Baum, L. F. (2005). *15 Books in 1: L. Frank Baum's Original 'Oz' Series*. Shoes and Ships and Sealing Wax, Ltd. (original works published 1908–20).

Beauvoir, S. (1974). *The Second Sex* (H. M. Parshley, trans.). New York: Vintage Books (original work published in French in 1949).

Butler, J. (1990). *Gender Trouble: Feminism and the Subversion of Identity*. New York: Routledge.

Butler, J. (1993). 'Imitation and gender insubordination'. In H. Abelove, M. A. Barale, and D. M. Halperin (eds), *The Lesbian and Gay Studies Reader*, pp.307–20. New York: Routledge.

Cixous, H. (2008). 'Sorties'. In D. Lodge and N. Wood (eds), *Modern Criticism and Theory: A Reader* (3rd ed.), pp.359–65. Malaysia: Pearson Education.

Cochran, G. and Harpending, H. (2009). *The 10,000 Year Explosion: How Civilization Accelerated Human Evolution*. New York: Basic Books.

Dupré, J. (1993). *The Disorder of Things: Metaphysical Foundations of the Disunity of Science*. Cambridge, MA: Harvard University Press.

Feinberg, L. (1993). *Stone Butch Blues*. San Francisco: Firebrand Books.

Feinberg, L. (1996). *Transgender Warriors: Making History from Joan of Arc to Dennis Rodman*. Boston: Beacon Press.

Feinberg, L. (1998). *Trans Liberation: Beyond Pink or Blue*. Boston: Beacon Press.

Feinberg, L. (2006). *Drag King Dreams*. New York : Carroll & Graf.

Frye, M. (1996). 'The necessity of differences: Constructing a positive category of Women'. *Signs 21*(4), 991–1010.

Hale, J. (n.d.). *Suggested Rules for Non-transsexuals Writing about Transsexuals, Transsexuality, Transsexualism, or Trans* ___. Retrieved 25 March 2010 from http://sandystone.com/hale.rules.html.

Jagose, A. (1996). *Queer Theory: An Introduction*. New York: NYU Press.

Kornblith, H. (1993). *Inductive Inference and its Natural Ground*. Cambridge, MA: MIT Press.

Lewis, M. (1975). 'Early sex differences in the human: Studies of socioemotional development'. *Archives of Sexual Behavior*, 4(4), 329–35.

Lorber, J. (1994). 'Night to his day: The social construction of gender'. In *Paradoxes of Gender*, pp.13–36. New Haven: Yale University Press.

Mishra, V., Roy, T. K., and Retherford, R. D. (2004). 'Sex differentials in childhood feeding, health care and nutritional status'. *Population and Development Review*, 30(2), 269–95.

Moulton, Janice (1977). 'The myth of the neutral "man"'. In M. Vetterling-Braggin, F. A. Elliston, and J. English (Eds.), *Feminism and Philosophy*, pp. 124–37. Totowa, NJ: Littlefield Adams.

Pande, R. (2003). 'Selective gender differences in childhood nutrition and immunization in rural India: The role of siblings'. *Demography*, 40(3), 395–418.

Piercy, M. (1976). *Woman on the Edge of Time*. New York: Alfred A. Knopf.

Plato (1991). *The Republic* (B. Jowett, trans.). New York: Vintage Books (original work written c.380 BCE)

Spruijt-Metz, D., Li, C., Cohen, E., Birch, L., and Goran, M. (2006). 'Longitudinal influence of mother's child-feeding practices on adiposity in children'. *The Journal of Pediatrics*, 148(3), 314–20.

Warren, V. L., American Philosophical Association, Committee on the Status of Women in the Profession (1986). 'Guidelines for the nonsexist use of language'. *Proceedings and Addresses of the American Philosophical Association*, 59(3), 471–84.

Notes

1 Or, perhaps, there lurks a fear that the elimination of such distinctions would also eliminate the privilege they provide to members of dominant groups.

2 Identity politics is used in reference to political and theoretical activity based on solidarity among members of the same identity category, such as gender, race, or ethnicity.

3 Existentialism usually refers to a philosophical school of thought associated with Jean-Paul Sartre, Simone de Beauvoir, and many others, particularly during the first half of the 20th century. Although there is a great deal of variation from one theorist to the next, a common thread running through the different perspectives is the search for meaning in a causally determined physical world.

4 Gender ultimately derives from the same root as 'genus' and refers to 'kind' or 'sort'.

5 Because it is also possible that the recognition of certain genital structures as female and others as male is itself socially negotiated, some people believe that, not just gender, but both sex and gender are socially constructed.

6 While most cultural feminists, as well as many proponents of the ethics of care and some proponents of ecofeminism, seem to accept the proposition that women are inherently more nurturing than men, many others, particularly many liberal feminists, would likely disagree. The continuities and discontinuities among various articulations of feminism are addressed in Chapter 7.

7 The creation of new breeds is ongoing, as demonstrated by the recent

recognition of the Irish red and white setter by the American Kennel Club in 2009 and the Westminster Kennel Club in 2010.

8 It is widely accepted that all dog breeds descended from wolves through many, many generations of domestication and breeding for various characteristics.

9 A heuristic is a problem-solving procedure or technique that is valued for its practical utility, even if it lacks complete accuracy or precision.

10 For a thorough discussion of the limitations of the allegedly generic use of masculine terms, refer to Janice Moulton's 'Myth of the Neutral "Man"' (Moulton, 1977).

11 Leslie Feinberg is the author of the novel *Stone Butch Blues* (1993) as well as more theoretical analyses, including *Transgender Warriors: Making History from Joan of Arc to Dennis Rodman* (1996); *Trans Liberation: Beyond Pink or Blue* (1998); and *Drag King Dreams* (2006). More information about Leslie Feinberg is available at http://transgenderwarrior.blogspot.com.

12 While many find the disagreement in number between singular subjects and the plural pronouns 'they' and 'their' insufferable, others are quite comfortable with this increasingly common usage, particularly in informal contexts.

13 And even more specifically, what comes to mind is a white, European or north-American, formally educated, upper middle-class, able-bodied, Christian, heterosexual man who also conforms to the dominant ideal along even more dimensions of identity. Eventually, when enough additional dimensions of identity come to mind, however, what emerges is the irony that the generic 'everyman' to which these allegedly generic terms purport to refer is quite rare, if he even exists at all.

14 Essentialism, which is discussed in more detail in Chapter 1, is usually used in reference to the belief that particular things can be organized into general categories based not on mere convenience or human invention but rather on characteristics that define the individual category members at the most fundamental level.

15 A commitment to natural kinds does not necessarily entail a commitment to essentialism. For a notable exception, consider John Dupré's 'promiscuous realism', according to which nature divides into many overlapping sets of real kinds. Because this account means that things can belong simultaneously to multiple natural kind categories, nothing is fully definable by reference to any one category in particular (Dupré, 1993).

16 The term hegemony refers to power, particularly of a state, that exerts a controlling influence over others. Often this influence is so strong that it seems natural and, as a result, goes unnoticed.

17 The theory of the Forms is sometimes translated from the original ancient Greek as the Theory of Ideas.

18 An early analysis of the totalizing character of binary thinking is found in Helene Cixous' 'Sorties' (2008, p.63) which presents a range of paired opposites, such as activity and passivity, sun and moon, culture and nature, day and night, father and mother, head and heart, and so on, as expressions of the same binary mode of thought.

7

Feminism Examined
and Explored

'Now you've got your diploma, Em,' said Uncle Henry, with a laugh, 'and I'm glad of it. This is a queer country, and we may as well take people as we find them.'
(L. Frank Baum, *The Emerald City of Oz*, p.225)

Feminist Thought and Action

The notion of gender as performance (Butler, 1990; Lorber, 1994) serves as a reminder that gender is not simply about language and thought, but it is also about action and lived experience. Gender is not theory removed from practice, nor is feminism just an academic exercise. Feminism exists not just in response to but also in the form of the lived experiences of real people. The thoughts and actions of those engaged in feminist social and political movements affect the discourses produced by those engaged in feminist scholarship within women's studies and related academic disciplines, and vice versa. The people engaged in feminist social and political movements and the people engaged in feminist scholarship are sometimes, in fact, the same people.

Feminism as a social and political movement, particularly within the USA, is often represented with the metaphor of waves that swell and retreat depending on the level of enthusiasm and need for feminist intervention. The first wave of the women's movement is usually associated with the suffrage movement that culminated in the passage of the 19th amendment giving US women the legal right to vote in 1920. The second wave is associated with what is often referred to as the women's liberation movement, which led to a number of legal and social developments, including an increase in women in the paid workforce and increased attention to the problem of violence against women. Although there is some disagreement about whether or not the second wave is over, those who believe that a third wave has begun often associate it with pluralism and the celebration of variation among people in general, and among women in particular.

Many of the texts associated with the first wave are taken from the political realm, particularly in the form of speeches and editorials. Although there was no shortage of political writing during the second wave, the second wave also witnessed the birth of women's studies as an academic discipline in much of the western world. This was accompanied by a predictable increase in scholarly attention to feminist questions. The distinction between sex and gender, which is still regarded as a core concept within women's studies and related fields, invites at least two such questions. The first question asks whether women and men are biological or social phenomena, and the second asks whether women and men are fundamentally the same or fundamentally different. These are closely related questions. If women and men are regarded as fundamentally the same, then this would suggest that any differences that exist are accidental, or learned differences. If what it means to be a woman or a man is learned then women and men are fundamentally the same in terms of biology. In a world without gender, or at least without gender socialization, would people be more like the androgynous characters that inhabit the fictional future imagined in Marge Piercy's 1976 novel *Woman on the Edge of Time?*[1]

This tension between sameness and difference is an important issue within feminist scholarship. In their 2006 reader, *Theorizing Feminisms*, Elizabeth Hackett and Sally Haslanger identify three general approaches for theorizing sex oppression. These include the 'sameness' approach, also described as humanist feminism, and the 'difference' approach, also described as gynocentric feminism.[2] The sameness approach is referred to as humanist presumably on the basis of an underlying assumption that, because women and men are fundamentally the same, it is unnecessary to differentiate between them. In other words, respect for humans in general ultimately amounts to respect for women in particular.[3] These two models are not the only way of characterizing conceptual differences among the various theoretical approaches collected under the banner of feminism. For example, Hackett and Haslanger also acknowledge a third perspective, namely the 'dominance' approach, which abandons questions about sameness and difference to concentrate instead on the subordination of women.

This conceptual space can also be divided along different boundaries. For example, where Hackett and Haslanger refer to the tension between sameness and difference, or between humanist and gynocentric versions of feminism, others employ the more familiar labels, liberal feminism and cultural feminism. Where Hackett and Haslanger refer to the dominance approach, others refer to radical feminism. Tong's *Feminist Thought* (1989, 1998, 2008) and Jaggar and Rothenberg's *Feminist Frameworks*

(1978, 1984, 1993) are two influential surveys of the recent history of feminist scholarship. The 1989 edition of *Feminist Thought* divides the field into liberal feminism, radical feminism, Marxist feminism, cultural feminism, psychoanalytic feminism, socialist feminism, existentialist feminism, and postmodern feminism. The 1998 edition made a few changes, and the 2008 update made even more. Tong's current inventory of the various positions within feminism includes liberal feminism, radical feminism, Marxist and socialist feminism, psychoanalytic feminism, care-centred feminism; multicultural, global, and postcolonial feminism; ecofeminism; and, finally, postmodern and third-wave feminism. Jaggar and Rothenberg's *Feminist Frameworks* provides a similarly updated set of categories with each new edition, but it has not been updated since 1993, when it referred only to liberal feminism, Marxist feminism, radical feminism, socialist feminism, multicultural feminism, and global feminism. Finally, in a noteworthy article in *Bitch Magazine*, Rachel Fudge (2006) offered an account of the major trends within feminist scholarship and activism.[4] According to Fudge, the major trends within feminism include liberal feminism, radical feminism, cultural feminism (which is also identified as essentialist feminism or difference feminism), and third-wave feminism.

As suggested by the differences among various publications, and even across editions of the same publications, the proposed categories for distinguishing the various forms of feminism do not represent all perspectives equally well. Such categories are nevertheless useful for organizing the otherwise diverse body of literature loosely collected under the banner of feminism. Assuming that the areas of greatest overlap among the different categories can be taken as evidence of their widespread acceptance and well-established significance, the noteworthy forms of feminist theory would seem to include *liberal feminism*, *Marxist feminism*, *radical feminism*, and *socialist feminism*, and it would also seem that the field is expanding to include *multicultural feminism* and *global feminism* as well.

So far, 'feminist theory' has been used in reference to theorizing that addresses feminist questions and concerns. A closely related sort of theorizing that is also relevant to the present discussion is feminist philosophy, whereby a feminist perspective, attitude, or orientation is applied to philosophical questions and concerns. Feminist *ethics*, in which a feminist perspective is applied to the study of morality, and feminist *epistemology*, in which a feminist perspective is applied to the study of knowledge, are two examples. The two schools of thought most commonly identified as uniquely feminist ways of thinking about ethics are the *ethics of care* and *ecofeminism*. To identify the schools of thought most commonly identified as feminist ways of thinking about epistemology, it may be useful to turn to Sandra Harding's 'Rethinking Standpoint Epistemology: What is "Strong" Objectivity?' (1993) and

Donna Haraway's 'Situated Knowledges: The Science Question in Feminism and the Privilege of Partial Perspective' (1991). Both essays mark a distinction between feminist empiricism and feminist standpoint theory.

Finally, postmodern feminism and third-wave feminism both have been associated with feminist theory, feminist ethics, and feminist epistemology, and both warrant some discussion. With the addition of postmodern feminism and third-wave feminism, the inventory of the various articulations of feminism now includes *liberal feminism*, *Marxist feminism*, *radical feminism*, *socialist feminism*, *multicultural feminism*, *global feminism*, *ethics of care*, *ecofeminism*, *feminist empiricism*, *feminist standpoint theory*, *postmodern feminism*, and finally *third-wave feminism*.

Feminist Theory

Two classic pieces set the tone for much of the early feminist literature. These include Mary Wollstonecraft's *A Vindication of the Rights of Woman* (1967), originally published in 1792, and John Stuart Mill's 'The Subjection of Women' (1970), originally published in 1869. Rooted in political liberalism, liberal feminism presupposes a universal rationality such that good, careful reasoning is all that is needed in order to establish social justice. Like political liberalism, liberal feminism denies that accident of birth is sufficient to justify an inequitable distribution of good, including such intangible goods as rights and opportunities. By rejecting the notion that nature warrants the subordinate status of women, liberal feminism gives birth to the distinction between sex and gender. According to liberal feminism, sexism is the product of bad reasoning, and the goal of feminism is to make the necessary corrections, particularly within the legal system. John Stuart Mill explains the proper role of reason, rather than prejudice, in determining the proper treatment of women:

> The least that can be demanded is, that the question should not be considered as prejudged by existing fact and existing opinion, but open to discussion on its merits, as a question of justice and expediency: the decision on this, as on any of the other social arrangements of mankind, depending on what an enlightened estimate of tendencies and consequences may show to be most advantageous to humanity in general, without distinction of sex. And the discussion must be a real discussion, descending to foundations, and not resting satisfied with vague and general assertions. It will not do, for instance to assert in general terms, that the experience of mankind has pronounced in favour of the

existing system. Experience cannot possibly have decided between two courses, so long as there has only been experience of one. If it be said that the doctrine of the equality of the sexes rests only on theory, it must be remembered that the contrary doctrine also has only theory to rest upon.

(Mill, 1970, p.147)

It is worth noting that Alice Walker (1983) articulated womanism as alternative to the white, sometimes even racist, orientation of mainstream feminism. Rachel Fudge lists womanism under the larger heading of liberal feminism, presumably because womanism shares with liberal feminism an interest in liberation strategies. The difference, however, is that womanism, unlike liberal feminism, addresses *intersectionality*. Intersectionality refers to the simultaneous impact of race, gender, and class on the lives of Black women (Davis, 1981; Crenshaw, 1994).

A frequent criticism of liberal feminism addresses the ideals of equality and autonomy associated with liberalism. Consider divorce law, for example. At a time when wage labour was impractical for the vast majority of white, middle class and upper-middle class US and European housewives, due to lack of relevant training and social pressure to stay at home, alimony was critical for the survival of most divorced women. Accordingly, early feminists supported legal measures aimed at creating genuine opportunities for women to escape bad marital situations. In the context of an ideology based on autonomy and equality, however, to identify women, or at least housewives, as a class of people in need of special legal protection denies their status as equal and autonomous members of society.

Dissatisfaction with liberal feminism invites an analysis of the structural constraints contributing to the subordination of women, particularly capitalism. Just as Marxism identifies capitalism as the source of oppression, Marxist feminism (for example Reed, 1970) identifies capitalism as the source of women's oppression. On this account, the role of women within contemporary western society is rooted not in biology but in the rise of capitalism. From this perspective, the remedy is obvious. Although women have traditionally done most of the domestic labour, this labour goes unacknowledged by a social system that presupposed the economic dependence of women on men. Women need power, which derives from economic leverage. Marxist feminism therefore advocates the socialization of domestic labour or the more thorough integration of women into the wage labour system.

Marxist feminism has been criticized for reducing women's oppression to a subcategory of economic oppression. In a now famous analysis of rape, Catharine MacKinnon (1987) addresses the limitations of both liberal and Marxist approaches to feminism. On an economic model, rape is construed as an issue of property rights. Sex becomes rape only when it occurs as an act of wrongful possession between a man and a woman to whom he is not sexually entitled. The legal distinction between rape and consensual sex, according to MacKinnon, fosters this interpretation. It reinforces the role of men as those who seek a commodity, namely sex, that is owned by women (or their fathers, husbands, brothers, and other protectors). MacKinnon claims that, by differentiating between sex and rape, some feminist analyses inadvertently perpetuate a system of sexual violence against women. For this reason, MacKinnon adopts radical feminism and advocates voluntary lesbianism as an alternative to the power symmetry inherent in heterosexual relationships.

Adrienne Rich also advocates voluntary lesbianism, which is used almost interchangeably with woman-identification, as an alternative to the oppressive system that enforces the heterosexual norm:

> Woman-identification is a source of energy, a potential springhead of female power, violently curtailed and wasted under the institution of heterosexuality. The denial of reality and visibility to women's passion for women, women's choice of women as allies, life companions, and community; the forcing of such relationships into dissimulation and their disintegration under intense pressure have meant an incalculable loss to the power of all women to change the social relations of the sexes, to liberate ourselves and each other. The lie of compulsory female heterosexuality today afflicts not just feminist scholarship, but every profession, every reference work, every curriculum, every organizing attempt, every relationship or conversation over which it hovers. It creates, specifically, a profound falseness, hypocrisy, and hysteria in the heterosexual dialogue, for every heterosexual relationship is lived in the queasy strobelight of that lie. However we choose to identify ourselves, however we find ourselves labeled, it flickers across and distorts our lives.
>
> (Rich, 1980, p.657)

While not all radical feminists oppose heterosexuality, they do tend to agree that it is historically and socially problematic (for example Bunch, 1975; Rich, 1980). This is because heterosexual relationships often perpetuate *patriarchy*. Patriarchy is best characterized as a social structure that grants priority to that which is male or masculine over that which is female or feminine. Various articulations of radical feminism are unified by their mutual critique of patriarchy as the fundamental source of sexism.

Socialist feminism emerges as something of a synthesis of Marxist and radical feminisms. Socialist feminism opposes the primacy of class in Marxist analyses and of sex in radical analyses, and instead regards capitalism and male sexual dominance as equal partners in the subordination of women (for example Hartmann, 1981). For this reason, it is believed that socialist reform is necessary, but that reform efforts will be adequate only if they address the often hidden female half of the labour force. According to socialist feminism, lower classes of men are simultaneously privileged and disadvantaged. They possess power in relation to women, but they lack power in the larger social context. Since men have no immediate or obvious interest in relinquishing power over women, socialist reform will be insufficient unless it is also feminist.

Finally, multicultural and global feminisms both exhibit interest in, and respect for, the lived experiences of women who are outside the mainstream culture of white Americans and Europeans. Multicultural feminism (for example Collins, 1990; Anzaldua, 1987), also sometimes referred to as 'women of colour feminism', addresses the unique issues that racial and ethnic minority women experience as a result of the intersecting influences of gender, race, class, and sexuality on cultural identities.[5] Consider, for example, Anzaldua's discussion of the dual identity developed as a Mestiza, or border dweller:

As a *mestiza* I have no country, my homeland cast me out; yet all countries are mine because I am every woman's sister or potential lover. (As a lesbian I have no race, my own people disclaim me; but I am all races because there is the queer of me in all races.)
(Anzaldua, 1987, p.80)

Global feminism (for example Mies, 1986; Enloe, 1995) represents a broader perspective which regards the lives of all women as inextricably interconnected, regardless of their geographic and political separation. In particular, global feminism examines the impact of imperialism and colonialism, thereby bringing international politics to the analysis of women's issues. Consider, for instance, Cynthia Enloe's (1995) influential article 'The Globetrotting Sneaker', which exposed the impact on people in general, but particularly on women and their children, when multinational corporations like Nike exploit the workers and natural resources in vulnerable parts of the world.

Despite an unmistakable solidarity among those interested in feminist theory and those interested in lesbian and gay rights, there are significant conceptual tensions between the feminist theory produced by the second wave and some of the ideas associated with traditional lesbian and gay studies. The liberal feminism of the second wave employs a conception of rights borrowed from liberal political theory. According to liberal feminism, women and men are fundamentally the same and should, therefore, be afforded the same rights and opportunities. Among the first to differentiate between sex as a matter of biology and gender as a product of society, second-wave liberal feminists argue that the vast majority of observable differences between the sexes are learned rather than innate. According to this position, the only thing that separates women and men is the sex organs. The effectiveness of this position as a foundation for equality of rights and opportunities is made especially clear by Gloria Steinem's oft-quoted claim that, 'There are very few jobs that actually require a penis or vagina – all others should be open to everyone.'

Like liberal feminism, the contemporary lesbian and gay rights movement aims to secure equality of rights and opportunities regardless of differences in sexuality. Just as liberal feminists argue that women and men are fundamentally the same, separated only by sex organs, many lesbian and gay rights activists likewise argue that homosexuals and heterosexuals, separated only by sexuality, are fundamentally the same.

Whereas liberal feminism invokes socialization as the underlying cause of most differences between women and men, the lesbian and gay rights movement rejects socialization as a determining factor in the case of sexual orientation. Thus, where liberal feminism regards biological determinism with suspicion, the lesbian and gay rights movement often endorses it.

One interpretation of the slogan 'the personal is political', commonly attributed to second-wave feminists, is that social acceptance of domestic violence can be reversed only by drawing attention to such problems. In other words, what happens behind closed doors is not merely a private matter, but rather an extension of the social inequalities between women and men. In contrast, lesbian and gay rights activists often argue that what happens behind closed doors is strictly a private matter. According to second-wave feminism, intimate relationships are of public and political concern; according to the lesbian and gay rights movement, they are private and personal.

Another interpretation of 'the personal is political', associated with the more radical feminism of the second wave, is that social institutions, most notably compulsory heterosexuality, perpetuate and reinforce the oppression of women by men. On this position, heterosexuality should be rejected in favour of voluntary lesbianism. Lesbian existence is regarded as something that can and should be chosen as a form of political resistance. This runs counter to the virtually unanimous agreement within the lesbian and gay rights movement that sexual orientation is innate, rather than something that involves an element of choice. The lesbian and gay rights movement maintains that identities are biological and sexual orientation is involuntary. For many second-wave feminists, however, identities are socialized, and for many second-wave radical feminists, sexual orientation is voluntary.[6]

Feminist Philosophy

Unlike feminist theory, which takes as its starting point the goal of eliminating or otherwise addressing sexism and its underlying causes, feminist philosophy in the more general sense addresses the same sorts of issues addressed by mainstream philosophy, such as ethics. In the early 1980s, research by Carol Gilligan (1982), Nel Noddings (1984), and others suggested that girls and women may be disposed toward a different style of ethical reasoning than boys and men. Specifically, they suggested that ethics based on the natural impulse to care for others provides a feminine and feminist alternative to more familiar systems of ethics that are based on notions of justice. One concern raised in connection with the ethics of care is its apparent commitment to gender essentialism. A related concern is that, by linking women with care, it reinforces the historical relegation of women to domestic labour performed largely as a service to others.

Although the ethics of care has fallen out of favour somewhat, especially when compared to its overwhelming popularity in the late 1980s and early 90s, there is still a great deal of interest in finding alternatives to traditional approaches to ethics, which have tended to concentrate on the use of reason by individual moral agents. The two most commonly referenced positions within traditional ethics are deontological ethics, especially in the example of the German philosopher Immanuel Kant's *Groundwork of the Metaphysics of Morals* (1998), first published in 1785,[7] and teleological ethics, especially in the example of the utilitarian position advanced by John Stuart Mill (2001) in 1863.[8] Kant and Mill provide different rules for differentiating between conduct that is morally right and conduct that is morally wrong, but they both agree that there are universal rules by which to differentiate between conduct that is morally right and conduct that is morally wrong. In addition, both Kant and Mill, like most philosophers working within the contemporary western tradition, regard morality as the achievement of individuals making personal choices in the face of moral dilemmas. The ethics of care offers an alternative account in which morality is situated in relationships as a whole, rather than in discreet choices and actions or the moral rules that govern those choices and actions.

Like the ethics of care, ecofeminism resists the temptation to supply universal moral rules, and seeks instead to reveal and address what Karen Warren (2000) refers to as 'the logic of domination' in the relationships between people or groups of people, and also in the relationships between people or groups of people and other parts of the natural world:

According to ecological feminists ('ecofeminists'), important connections exist between the treatment of women, people of color, and the underclass on one hand and the treatment of nonhuman nature on the other. Ecological feminists claim that any feminism, environmentalism, or environmental ethic which fails to take these connections seriously is grossly inadequate. Establishing the nature of these connections, particularly what I call women-nature connections, and determining which are potentially liberating for both women and nonhuman nature is a major project of ecofeminist philosophy.

(Warren, 1997, p.3)

The ecofeminist critique of the logic of domination is ultimately a critique of the western philosophical tradition, which has devoted itself to establishing the superiority of reason, and hence of humankind, in the specific form of mankind, over everything else.

Feminist epistemology provides an additional critique of contemporary western ideas about the power and scope of human reason and rationality. In order to understand this critique, however, it is important to have a basic understanding of traditional epistemology, particularly logical positivism. Logical empiricism, sometimes referred to as logical positivism, describes the union of positivism, or empiricism, and logic. Positivism is the belief that statements are meaningful only if they are verifiable through experience. Logic is a system for analysing the formal relationships between and among statements. Logical empiricism thus refers to an account whereby knowledge, especially scientific knowledge, is produced when empirically verifiable data, in the form of observation statements, are subjected to logical analysis in order to confirm or disconfirm a range of theories and hypotheses. This account presupposes that it is both possible and desirable for scientists and other epistemic agents to be neutral in the collection and evaluation of data, such that a given epistemic agent is, or at least should be, virtually interchangeable with any other epistemic agent.

Feminist empiricism shares with logical empiricism a commitment to scientific neutrality, but denies that sexism and other forms of bias are easily avoided. Feminist empiricists have exposed numerous cases in which predominantly male scientific communities have misrepresented or ignored women and, as result, have generated faulty conclusions. For instance, the exclusive use of male subjects in experiments intended for generalization to the larger human population is no longer deemed acceptable, largely because feminist empiricists have revealed the hidden biases of this practice. Indeed, the ethics of care emerged as an alternative traditional ethics precisely because feminist research on moral development in children revealed that earlier work had concentrated almost exclusively on boys. According to feminist empiricism, sexist science occurs when scientists fail to reason as carefully and neutrally as they should. Thus, the role of feminist empiricism is largely corrective.

Critics of feminist empiricism note that careless reasoning is not the only problem in science that feminism must address. Consider, for example, the accusation that, throughout recent history, medical science has devoted more resources to the health care needs of men than to the health care needs of women. While this does not suggest that scientists have reasoned badly, it does suggest that good reasoning alone may be insufficient to ensure scientific neutrality. Whereas feminist empiricism reiterates the traditional claim that all rational agents are epistemologically equal, standpoint theory (as represented, for example in Harding, 2003) suggests that social boundaries can act as epistemic boundaries, and epistemic agents will seek only the sorts of knowledge to which they have access. Standpoint theory borrows from Marxism the suggestion that those living under conditions of domination have a more complete perspective than their oppressors (Smith, 1987, pp.78–88). On this account, epistemic communities consist of a dominant group, or centre, and a dominated group, or margin (refer to Figure 7.1). From the margin, someone gains an outsider's perspective on the centre, and is thereby better equipped to expose the limitations of the dominant ideology. Using the physical boundary drawn by railroad tracks as a metaphor for the marginal social location of those outside the dominant group, bell hooks describes this dual perspective:

> To be in the margin is to be part of the whole but outside the main body. For black Americans living in a small Kentucky town, the railroad tracks were a daily reminder of our marginality. Across those tracks were paved streets, stores we could not enter, restaurants we could not eat in, and people we could not look directly in the face. Across those tracks was a world we could work in as maids, as janitors, as prostitutes, as long as it was in a service capacity. We could enter that world, but we could not live there. We had always to return to the margin, to beyond the tracks, to shacks and abandoned houses on the edge of town.
>
> There were laws to ensure our return. To not return was to risk being punished. Living as we did – on the edge – we developed a particular way of seeing reality. *We looked both from the outside in and from the inside out. We focused our attention on the center as well as on the margin. We understood both.* This mode of seeing reminded us of the existence of a whole universe, a main body made up of both margin and center. Our survival depended on an ongoing public awareness of the separation between margin and center and an ongoing private acknowledgment that we were a necessary, vital part of that whole.
>
> (hooks, 2000, p.xvi, emphasis added)

Like feminist empiricism, the role of standpoint theory is largely corrective. Again like feminist empiricism, standpoint theory implies that some perspectives are epistemologically preferable to others. Unlike feminist empiricism, however, standpoint theory indicates that the corrective, privileged perspective can be achieved only from the social margins.

Figure 7.1 Margin and centre

An important criticism of standpoint theory is that the dichotomy between insiders and outsiders, or the centre and the margin, is too simplistic. Feminist standpoint theory describes a social world in which the position of women is marginal to the position of men. But there are, of course, contexts in which the position of particular women is marginal to the position of other women, as well as contexts in which the position of particular men is marginal to the position of other men. Attention to race, class, sexuality, and other factors disrupts the notion that there is a straightforward boundary between insiders and outsiders. If the marginal perspective of women is generally preferable to the perspective of men, then it would seem that the more marginal perspective of Black women would be preferable to the perspective of white women, the more marginal perspective of poor Black women would be preferable to the perspective of middle-class or wealthy Black women, and so on.[9]

Instead of degenerating into debates over which groups are more marginal that others, many feminists simply acknowledge, first, that perspectives acquired as a result of social positioning impact the production of knowledge and, second, that epistemic communities can benefit from seeking input from multiple perspectives (for example Longino, 1990). Some prescribe multiple perspectives as a means of correcting the implicit biases of particular perspectives. Others suggest that multiple perspectives can work together to provide a more complete perspective. This approach, which can be usefully identified as perspectival pluralism, abandons the rigid dichotomy between insiders and outsiders associated with early versions of standpoint theory.

Like standpoint theories, postmodern feminism acknowledges that social positioning influences epistemological perspective. In order to understand postmodern feminism, it will be helpful first to have a basic understanding of postmodernism. In order to understand postmodernism, it will be helpful first to have a basic understanding of modernism. In everyday usage, 'modern' refers literally to whatever is new, whatever is happening at the current moment. In its more technical usage, 'modernism' refers to specific eras and schools of thought within a variety of different domains, such as philosophy, science studies, art history, literary criticism, film theory, and so on. What modernism means for science studies, for example, may have very little in common with what it means for art history or any other field. Addressing very briefly its usage in philosophy, the modern era began around the beginning of the 17th century, against the historical backdrop of the scientific revolution, and lasted into the beginning of the 19th century, in the context of the Enlightenment. The Enlightenment is perhaps best described as a general attitude of celebration and optimism about the potential use of reason to obtain truth and achieve the highest human potential. This optimism is precisely what postmodernism leaves behind.

For postmodernism in general, and for postmodern feminism in particular, there is no absolute truth. Any attempt to distinguish fact from fiction is thus a political project, based as much in ideology and values as it is in evidence and logic. For postmodern feminism, in which postmodernism is applied to the subject matter of feminism, this means that there is no underlying truth about sex or gender. In a particularly provocative statement of this position, Judith Butler has suggested not just that gender is socially constructed, but that sex itself is also socially constructed. Sex, Butler claims, 'is an ideal construct which is forcibly materialized through time. It is not a simple fact or static condition of a body, but a process whereby regulatory norms materialize "sex" and achieve this materialization through a forcible reiteration of those norms' (Butler, 1993, pp.1–2).

Queer Theory

There is quite a lot of overlap across the categories outlined above. There is an obvious connection between first-wave feminism, liberal feminism, and feminist empiricism. In each case, the proper role for feminism is to promote the diligent application of reason as a means to achieve truth and justice. There is also a connection between multicultural feminism and feminist standpoint theory. Both promote awareness of and appreciation for the social positioning of those outside the dominant mainstream identity categories. In yet another connection, ecofeminism and global feminism both address the impact of patriarchy on the experiences of women in the global context. Finally, in a connection that will be discussed in more detail in the Chapter 8, postmodern feminism overlaps with both third-wave feminism and queer theory.

Third-wave feminism describes the newest generations of feminists at a time in history when many have suggested that, at least for women in most of Europe and North America, feminism is no longer necessary. In fact, when Rebecca Walker referred to the 'third-wave' in 1992, thereby popularizing the term, it was in response to the suggestion in a *New York Times* article that a post-feminist era was underway (Baumgardner and Richards, 2000, p.77). While some challenge the notion of third-wave feminism by claiming that the second wave was successful enough that sexism is no longer a significant problem, others challenge the notion of third-wave feminism by claiming that the second wave has not yet completed its work.[10]

Figure 7.2 Rubin's sex hierarchy: the charmed circle vs. the outer limits

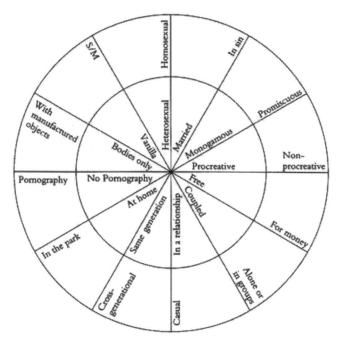

Source: Rubin, 1992, p.281

Third-wave feminism is not easily defined, partly because it is still in the process of establishing itself, and partly because one of the features common across different articulations of third-wave feminism is its recognition that there are multiple versions of what it means to be a feminist, or even a third-wave feminism. In fact, one common thread that connects postmodern feminism, third-wave feminism, and queer theory is the concern than an attempt to define something is ultimately an attempt to exert control. As depicted by Gayle Rubin's 'charmed circle' (refer to Figure 7.2), the process of defining sex is also the process of controlling it through the simultaneous formation of a distinction between sex that is 'normal' and sex that is 'deviant'. Depicted as a circle with a dominant core and an exterior margin, Rubin's charmed circle is reminiscent of the depiction of marginal and central social positions associated with feminist standpoint theory (refer to Figure 7.1). At the centre are socially prescribed sexual activities and practices, surrounded on the margins by socially prohibited sexual activities and practices.

In a published conversation between Judith Butler and Gayle Rubin, Rubin explained that this analysis developed partly as a response to feminist articulations of the difference between acceptable and unacceptable sexual activities and practices, many of which drove a wedge between feminists and gay men.

> Feminism was also used quite a bit as the political theory of gay male politics, and it didn't work very well. Very little gay male behavior actually was granted the feminist seal of approval. Most of the actual practice of gay male culture was objectionable to many feminists, who mercilessly condemned drag and cross-dressing, gay public sex, gay male promiscuity, gay male masculinity, gay leather, gay fist-fucking, gay cruising, and just about everything else gay men did. I could not accept the usual lines about why all this stuff was terrible and anti-feminist, and thought they were frequently an expression of reconstituted homophobia.
>
> (Rubin, as interviewed by Butler, 1994, pp.76)

Rubin recognizes that gender, sex, and sexuality are intimately connected. Indeed, it was Rubin (1975) who first referred to the 'sex-gender system' to describe 'the set of arrangements by which a society transforms biological sexuality into products of human activity, and in which these transformed sexual needs are satisfied' (Rubin, 1975, p.159). What this example demonstrates is that directing attention to all three of the interrelated concepts of gender, sex, and sexuality reveals forms of bias that might otherwise go unnoticed and unchallenged. In addition, this example invites an exploration of possible alternatives to the existing system of gender, sex, and sexuality.

Additional Resources

- Kolata, G. (1992). 'Who is female? Science can't say'. *The New York Times.* 16 February 1992.
- Saner, E. (2008). 'The gender trap'. *The Guardian.* 30 July 30 2008.
- Rich, A. (1980). 'Compulsory heterosexuality and lesbian existence'. *Signs: Journal of Women in Culture and Society,* 5(4) 647–50.
- Fudge, R. (2006). 'Everything you always wanted to know about feminism but were afraid to ask'. *Bitch Magazine,* 31, 58–67. Available online at http://bitchmagazine.org/article/everything-about-feminism
- Butler, J. (1994). 'Interview with Gayle Rubin: Sexual traffic'. *Differences: A Journal of Feminist Cultural Studies* 6(2–3), 62–98.
- Anderson, J., Coolidge, M., and Heche, A. (2000). *If These Walls Could Talk 2.* HBO Films.
- Query, J. (2000). *Live Nude Girls Unite.* Constant Communication.

References

Anderson, J., Coolidge, M., and Heche, A. (2000). *If These Walls Could Talk 2.* HBO Films.

Anzaldua, G. (1987). *Borderlands/La Frontera: The New Mestiza.* San Francisco: Aunt Lute.

Anzaldua, G. and Moraga, C. (eds) (1981). *This Bridge Called My Back: Writings by Radical Women of Color.* Watertown, MA: Persephone Press.

Baum, L. F. (2005). *15 Books in 1: L. Frank Baum's Original 'Oz' Series.* Shoes and Ships and Sealing Wax, Ltd. (original works published 1908–20).

Baumgardner, J. and Richards, A. (2000). *Manifesta: Young Women, Feminism, and the Future.* New York: Farrar, Straus and Giroux.

Bunch, C. (1975). 'Lesbians in revolt'. In *Lesbianism and the Women's Movement,* pp.29–37. Oakland, CA: Diana Press.

Butler, J. (1990). *Gender Trouble: Feminism and the Subversion of Identity.* New York: Routledge.

Butler, J. (1993). *Bodies That Matter: On the Discursive Limits of 'Sex'.* New York: Routledge.

Butler, J. (1994). 'Interview with Gayle Rubin: Sexual traffic'. *Differences: A Journal of Feminist Cultural Studies* 6(2–3), 62–98.

Collins, P. H. (1990). *Black Feminist Thought: Knowledge, Consciousness, and the Politics of Empowerment.* New York: Routledge.

Crenshaw, K. W. (1994). 'Mapping the margins: Intersectionality, identity politics, and violence against women of color'. In M. A. Fineman and R. Mykitiuk (eds), *The Public Nature of Private Violence,* pp.93–118. New York: Routledge.

Davis, A. Y. (1981). *Women, Race, and Class.* New York: Random House.

Enloe, C. (1995). 'The globetrotting sneaker'. *Ms. Magazine,* 5(5), p.10 (6 pages).

Fudge, R. (2006). 'Everything you always wanted to know about feminism but were afraid to ask'. *Bitch Magazine,* 31, 58–67.

Gilligan, C. (1982). *In a Different Voice: Psychological Theory and Women's Development.* Cambridge: Harvard University Press.

Hackett, E. and Haslanger, S. (eds) (2006). *Theorizing Feminisms: A Reader.* New York: Oxford University Press.

Haraway, D. (1991). 'Situated knowledges: The science question in feminism and the privilege of partial perspective'. In *Simians, Cyborgs, and Women: The Reinvention of Nature*, pp.183–201. New York: Routledge.

Harding, S. (1993). 'Rethinking standpoint epistemology: What is "strong" objectivity?'. In L. Alcoff and E. Potter (eds). *Feminist Epistemologies*, pp.49–82. New York: Routledge.

Harding, S. (ed.) (2003). *The Feminist Standpoint Theory Reader: Intellectual and Political Controversies.* New York: Routledge.

Hartmann, H. (1981). 'The unhappy marriage of Marxism and feminism: Towards a more progressive union'. In L. Sargent (ed.). *Women and Revolution*, pp.1–41. Boston: South End Press.

hooks, b. (2000). *Feminist Theory: From Margin to Center.* Boston: South End Press (original work published in 1984).

Jaggar, A. and Rothenberg, P. (eds). (1978, 1984, 1993). *Feminist Frameworks: Alternative Theoretical Accounts of the Relations between Women and Men.* New York: McGraw-Hill.

Kant, I. (1998). *Groundwork of the Metaphysics of Morals* (M. Gregor, trans.). Cambridge: Cambridge University Press (original work published in German in 1785).

Kolmar, W. and Bartkowski, F. (eds). (1999, 2003, 2009). *Feminist Theory: A Reader.* New York: McGraw-Hill.

Longino, H. (1990). *Science as Social Knowledge: Values and Objectivity in Scientific Inquiry.* Princeton: Princeton University Press.

Lorber, J. (1994). 'Night to his day: The social construction of gender'. In *Paradoxes of gender*, pp.13–36. New Haven: Yale University Press.

MacKinnon, C. (1987). 'Feminism, Marxism, method, and the state: Toward a feminist jurisprudence'. In S. Harding (ed.), *Feminism and Methodology*, pp.135–56. Bloomington and Indianapolis: Indiana University Press.

McCann, C. and Kim, S. (eds). (2002, 2009). *Feminist Theory Reader: Local and Global Perspectives.* New York: Routledge.

Mies, M. (1986). *Patriarchy and Accumulation on a World Scale: Women in the International Division of Labour.* London: Zed Books.

Mill, J. S. (1970). 'The subjection of women'. In A. Rossi (ed.), *Essays on Sex Equality: John Stuart Mill and Harriet Taylor Mill*, pp.125–56. Chicago: University of Chicago Press (original work published in 1869).

Mill, J. S. (2001). *Utilitarianism.* Indianapolis: Hackett (original work published in 1863).

Noddings, N. (1984). *Caring: A Feminine Approach to Ethics and Moral Education.* Berkeley: University of California Press.

Piercy, M. (1976). *Woman on the Edge of Time.* New York: Alfred A. Knopf.

Query, J. (2000). *Live Nude Girls Unite.* Constant Communication.

Reed, E. (1970). 'Women: Caste, class, or oppressed sex?'. In *Problems of Women's Liberation*, pp.64–76. New York: Pathfinder.

Rich, A. (1980). 'Compulsory heterosexuality and lesbian existence'. *Signs: Journal of Women in Culture and Society*, 5(4), 647–50.

Rubin, G. (1975). 'The traffic in women: Notes on the "political economy" of sex'. In R. R. Reiter (ed.), *Toward an Anthropology of Women*, pp.157–210. New York: Monthly Review, 1975.

Rubin, G. (1982, 1992). 'Thinking sex: Notes for a radical theory of the politics of sexuality'. In C. Vance (ed.), *Pleasure and Danger: Exploring Female Sexuality*, pp.267–319. London: Pandora Press.

Smith, D. (1987). *The Everyday World as Problematic: A Feminist Sociology*. Boston: Northeastern University Press.

Tong, R. (1989). *Feminist Thought: A Comprehensive Introduction*. Boulder, CO: Westview Press.

Tong, R. (1998, 2008). *Feminist Thought: A More Comprehensive Introduction*. Boulder, CO: Westview Press.

Walker, A. (1983). *In Search of Our Mothers' Gardens: Womanist Prose*. New York: Harcourt Brace Jovanovich.

Warren, K. J. (1997). 'Taking the empirical data seriously'. In K. J. Warren (ed.), *Ecofeminism: Women, Culture, Nature*, pp.3–20. Bloomington: Indiana University Press.

Warren, K. J. (2000). *Ecofeminist philosophy: A Western Perspective on What It Is and Why it Matters*. Lanham, MD: Rowman & Littlefield.

Weedon, C. (1987). *Feminist Practice and Poststructuralist Theory*. Cambridge, MA: Blackwell.

Wollstonecraft, M. (1967). *A Vindication of the Rights of Woman*. New York: Norton (original work published in 1792).

Notes

1 As discussed briefly in the previous chapter, Piercy's *Woman on the Edge of Time* (1976) goes into quite a bit of detail about how a society might function without implementing any gender roles or participating in any gender socialization, without differentiating between homosexuality and heterosexuality, and without attaching any stigma to sexual exploration, even among children.

2 Just as 'phallocentrism' refers to a bias that favours men, 'gynocentrism' refers to the adoption, often intentionally, of a bias that favours women.

3 This sense of humanism is distinct from its well-established usage as an alternative to religious perspectives.

4 *Bitch* is an independent magazine closely associated with third-wave feminism. For a more thorough introduction, visit http://bitchmagazine.org.

5 For an introduction to the work of multicultural feminists, refer to the collection *This Bridge Called My Back: Writings by Radical Women of Color* (Anzaldua and Moraga, 1981).

6 A vivid depiction of the tension in the USA during the 1970s, first, between lesbian feminists and other feminists and, second, between lesbian feminists and other lesbians, is available in the 2000 film *If These Walls Could Talk 2*, especially the second vignette, '1971'.

7 Briefly, Kant's deontological ethics suggests that morality consists in doing the right thing (namely, acting on principles that could consistently be universalized) for the right reason (because it is a duty, and not for any personal benefit).

8 Briefly, Mill's utilitarian ethics suggests that morality consists in maximizing happiness, or pleasure, and minimizing unhappiness, or pain, for everyone concerned.

9 For a discussion of the unique epistemological perspective of Black women, refer to Patricia Hill Collins (1990).

10 A vivid depiction of the tension between second-wave and third-wave feminist attitudes is available in the 2000 documentary film *Live Nude Girls Unite*, in which mother (Dr Joyce Wallace) and daughter (Julia Query, both feminist activists) exhibit different perspectives on the sex industry.

QUEER FEMINISM

Dorothy sighed and commenced to breathe easier. She began to realize that death was not in store for her, after all, but that she had merely started upon another adventure, which promised to be just as queer and unusual as were those she had before encountered.

(L. Frank Baum, *Dorothy and the Wizard in Oz*, p. 124)

8

Notes Toward a Queer Feminism

'Won't that make a queer combination?' inquired Kiki. 'The queerer the better,' declared Ruggedo.
(L. Frank Baum, *The Magic of Oz*, p.545)

The Intimate Connection between Queer and Feminist Theory

I am not the first to link queer theory and feminist theory. Even a cursory internet search will reveal various articles and pages dedicated to some variant of queer feminism. I do not believe that what I refer to as queer feminism is wholly original, however, nor do I believe that the development of new ideas is ever wholly original given the social character of knowledge production. Instead, I conceive of my project as part of a larger emerging trend situated at the intersection of feminism and queer theory.

What I refer to as queer feminism is simply the application of queer notions of gender, sex, and sexuality to the subject matter of feminist theory, and the simultaneous application of feminist notions of gender, sex, and sexuality to the subject matter of queer theory. Although the word 'queer' is commonly associated with sex and sexuality, queer theory is a way of understanding not just sex and sexuality but also gender. Specifically, queer theory avoids the binary and hierarchical reasoning usually associated with these concepts. Precisely what it is that constitutes the subject matter of feminism varies from one form of feminism to the next. Despite this diversity, however, almost every form of feminism addresses at least gender and sex, and sometimes sexuality as well. There is thus an implicit connection between queer theory and feminist theory, and queer feminism makes this connection more explicit.

Queer feminism brings both a queer orientation to feminist theory, and a feminist orientation to queer theory. Part of what makes the union of queer and feminist theory so inviting is that they already have much in common. As I have already noted, both address the intersecting issues of gender, sex, and sexuality. In the case of queer theory, however, the emphasis is on sex and sexuality. In the case of feminist theory, the emphasis is on gender and sex. An obvious outcome of uniting queer and feminist theory, then, is that the addition of a queer perspective promises to direct increased attention toward sexuality in the context of feminist theory, while the addition of a feminist perspective promises to direct increased attention to gender in the context of queer theory.

There are other concerns and consequences connected with the queering of feminism, of course, because queer theory does much more than simply accentuate sexuality. Because feminist theory does more than simply accentuate gender, there are likewise additional interests and issues associated with the explicit insertion of feminism into queer theory. The significance of bringing a queer orientation to feminist theory is addressed in the first section below, and the significance of bringing a feminist orientation to queer theory is addressed in the second section below.

The Queer in Queer Feminism

There is an unmistakable sense of solidarity linking concern about women's issues and concern about lesbian, gay, bisexual, and transgender issues. This solidarity seems to have more depth than the mere recognition that feminism must reflect the lives of women who identify as heterosexual as well as those who do not. This solidarity also seems to have more depth than the mere recognition that all people are entitled to equality of rights and opportunities. Instead, this solidarity seems born of a deep understanding that the oppression of women and the suppression of lesbian, gay, bisexual, and transgender existence are deeply intertwined. Feminist identity, like LGBT identity, stretches the boundaries of established categories of gender, sex, and sexuality.

Despite the implicit connection they share, there is a history of tension between feminist studies and sexuality studies, both in general and in the more specific case of queer theory. There is evidence of bias against lesbian women,[1] gay men,[2] bisexual people,[3] and transgender people[4] within the feminist canon. The explicit emphasis queer feminism places on sexuality can go a long way toward preventing such problems. A related issue is that there is also a history of racism and classism within the feminist canon.[5] Queer theory's critique of binary and hierarchical reasoning recognizes and addresses all forms of oppression as part of a logic of domination. The logic of domination is also a concern raised within ecofeminism, as discussed in Chapter 7. The logic of domination is a way of thinking about and interacting with the world and its inhabitants that is structured hierarchically in a manner that justifies the systematic subordination of those who lack power by those who possess it. The critique of the logic of domination offered by both some forms of feminism and queer theory promises to keep a check on racism, classism, and other expressions of oppression.

It is worth noting, however, that queer theory, like feminist theory, also has a history of racism and classism. What this suggests is that bias is pervasive, and a theoretical orientation that promises or aims to address a particular form of bias is never immune from perpetuating it. Not every critique that aims to attend to oppression will do so equally successfully. This realization can lead, especially initially, to a sense of despair regarding the possibility of avoiding or eliminating bias. At the same time, however, it can also serve as a reminder of how important it is to filter ideas through multiple disciplinary and personal screens. This process offers what may be our best chance of catching and removing as much of the residual debris of unintentional bias as possible. Indeed, the linking of queer and feminist perspectives layers yet another screen onto the filter. Because queer theory, and hence queer feminism, embraces multiplicity, there is no limit to this layering of screens in various combinations. Just as I am eager to integrate and articulate queer feminism, others have integrated and articulated queer perspectives on other fields as well.[6]

Another consequence of linking queer theory with feminism is that it signals a direction for feminism to take at a time when it seems to be searching for direction. In particular, it directs contemporary feminism, particularly third-wave feminism, away from a less appealing position that some, including Elizabeth Kissling (in Grigg-Spall, 2010), refer to as post-feminism. Kissling's reference to post-feminism is not intended to signal the end of feminism, but instead identifies the disingenuous process of 'taking feminism into account in order to dismiss it'. Post-feminism seems to suggest that the necessary conditions are already in place to achieve such feminist ideals as social and economic equality between women and men. Women simply need to take advantage of the opportunities already available. This is reminiscent of the attitude prevalent in the USA following the passage of the 19th amendment in 1920, which is often regarded as the culmination of the first wave of feminism. It was widely assumed that allowing women to vote put the necessary conditions in place to achieve such feminist ideals as social and economic equality. Women simply needed to exercise the elective franchise. They simply needed to make their choices. Similarly, post-feminism upholds the ability to make choices as emblematic of feminism. This is prevalent in popular western culture, and especially pronounced in the makeover genre of television programming and magazine copy, where freedom of expression among women is often reduced to the 'freedom', provided they have sufficient financial resources, for women to 'choose' a range of risky cosmetic surgeries. Casting this as an issue of free choice means missing the opportunity to critique the cultural conditions under which women are socialized to believe that our otherwise healthy bodies will never be sufficiently thin, curvy, tan, pale, tall, short, curly, straight, or whatever.

Post-feminism and third-wave feminism have some similarities, at least on the surface. This is not altogether surprising since both exist in response to, indeed as an alternative to, second-wave feminism. Recall, after all, that Rebecca Walker helped to popularize the expression, third wave, in response to a declaration in the *New York Times* that the feminist era was over and the post-feminist era had begun (Baumgardner and Richards, 2000, p.77). Indeed, both post-feminism and third-wave feminism take for granted that second-wave feminism has outlived its usefulness. For post-feminism, this is because it has already accomplished its mission, thus providing contemporary women with a wide range of options from which to make our precious choices. For the third wave, it is simply because second-wave feminism is outdated when compared with more contemporary approaches to dismantling patriarchy, such as those featured in the final section of this chapter. An important feature of post-feminism is that, whereas queer theory, third-wave feminism, and hence queer feminism provide a critical perspective on mainstream culture, post-feminism reinforces it by promoting choice, often consumer choice, masquerading under a façade of feminist expression. Queer feminism thus presents a welcome path toward the ongoing development of feminism as a critical perspective.

The Feminism in Queer Feminism

Just as there has been a history of bias against lesbian women, gay men, bisexual people, and transgender people within feminism, there also has been a history of bias against women within sexuality studies, including queer theory.[7] The explicit emphasis queer feminism places on gender is an obvious strategy toward preventing such problems. In addition, just as there has been a history of racism and classism in the feminist canon, there is likewise a history of racism and classism in the queer canon.[8] Once again, I suggest that the addition of another critical perspective, or the layering of additional screens can be useful in filtering out such biases as they occur.

Despite its value in addressing forms of oppression within queer theory, the pairing of the term feminism with the term queer is not at all unproblematic. One consequence of the radical critique of binary thinking that queer theory offers is that it seems to deny the reality of any categories, including not just categories of gender, such as feminine, but also categories of sex, such as female. If there are not really any females, if there is nothing that really is feminine, if there are no women, indeed not even any men, then there would seem to be little value in a theoretical perspective organized around sex and gender identity. Insofar as the term 'feminism' is referential of the existing sex and gender binaries, it might seem to be at odds with the rejection of binary forms of categorization.

Despite this apparent contradiction, I have chosen the problematic label 'queer feminism' intentionally, in full knowledge of the irony it exhibits. For one thing, I have learned enough from poststructuralism, and especially from Derrida,[9] to understand that, while meaning cannot be fixed permanently, it can be, indeed it must be, constantly negotiated for reference in particular contexts. This is how sexism, racism, and many other forms of oppression are able to function. Expectations and ideals are constantly revisited and revised, and this is part of what makes them so hard to achieve. Nevertheless, these expectations and ideals form the standards against which we are judged. In the response to sexism and racism, it is also necessary to recognize how the relevant meanings have been fixed relative to the oppressive contexts in which they are deployed. This is reminiscent of what Gayatri Spivak referred to in 1985 as 'strategic essentialism' (Spivak, 1996). Strategic essentialism is a strategy whereby groups with mutual goals and interests temporarily present themselves publicly as essentially the same for the sake of expediency and presenting a united front, while simultaneously engaging in ongoing and less public disagreement and debate.

Additionally, by using the term, I hope to draw attention to the problems inherent in the very notion of 'feminism'. Consistent with ideas from queer theory, it seems that present and past oppression of women, or any group, is ultimately attributable to binary thinking, which inevitably grants priority to the privileged side of the relevant binary. Thus, the concept of feminism is itself queer, in the sense of 'questionable' or 'suspicious', in that it reinforces the very problem it aims to resolve. Retaining 'feminism', however, reminds readers that, despite intentions to the contrary, the world just so happens to be structured in binary terms, and people assigned as female or feminine are often disadvantaged as a result. Until or unless the 'feminism' in 'queer feminism' is rendered meaningless through major linguistic and conceptual transformation, the 'feminism' in 'queer feminism' will remain relevant.

Emerging Queer Feminist Practices

Rather than closing with a clearly articulated conclusion, I offer instead a brief discussion of a few trends that are representative of what I take to be the spirit of queer feminism. In so doing, I hope that they might serve as inspiration for the ongoing development of queer feminism, not merely as an academic exercise, but as part of the lived experience. The examples I have selected are culture jamming, radical cheerleading, and zine making. My treatment of these topics is intentionally brief. My hope is that, following this quick introduction, at least some readers will continue to explore these practices, as well as the theoretical matters taken up throughout this book.

Culture jamming (Klein, 1999; Lasn, 2000) refers to a strategy for resisting consumerism and retaliating against corporate power through the use of clever stunts and pranks that deploy symbols and messages that are familiar from media and advertising, but alters them in ways that convey a more progressive or critical attitude. Klein explains an example of a particularly successful instance of culture jamming:

> Well, there's an upscale clothing company in London called Boxfresh. They decided to use images of the Zapatistas to sell their clothing. They put Subcommandante Marcos images in their windows. Some local activists decided this was not cool, so they dressed up like Zapatistas and started leafleting. They eventually got Boxfresh to agree to set up a computer terminal in the store where people could get information about who the Zapatistas actually are. They also got Boxfresh to agree to donate the profits from that particular line to the Zapatistas!
>
> (Quoted in Bullock, 2002)

Other examples are available on the pages of any issue of the magazine *Adbusters* or at their website, which is subtitled the 'Culturejammers Headquarters' (www.adbusters.org). Adbusters contains no advertising, though it often features artistic reworkings of many of the same advertising images featured on the pages of more mainstream magazines. Naomi Klein suggests that 'feminists were some of the original culture jammers' (quoted in Bullock, 2002), and this is clear in the case of the Guerrilla Girls. Their website, subtitled 'Fighting Discrimination with Facts, Humor and Fake Fur' (www.guerrillagirls.com), describes their activities:

> We're feminist masked avengers in the tradition of anonymous do-gooders like Robin Hood, Wonder Woman and Batman. How do we expose sexism, racism and corruption in politics, art, film and pop culture? With facts, humor and outrageous visuals. We reveal the understory, the subtext, the overlooked, the and the downright unfair....In the last few years, we've unveiled anti-film industry billboards in Hollywood just in time for the Oscars, and created large scale projects for the Venice Biennale, Istanbul and Mexico City. We dissed the Museum of Modern Art at its own Feminist Futures Symposium, examined the museums of Washington DC in a full page in the Washington Post, and exhibited large-scale posters and banners in Athens, Bilbao, Montreal, Rotterdam, Sarajevo and Shanghai.
>
> (www.guerrillagirls.com)

Radical cheeleading (Nedbalsky and Christmas, 2004) is like culture jamming in that it takes something familiar, in this case cheerleading, and turns it around to send a much different message, in this case a feminist political message. Radical cheerleading refers to groups of activists that form squads or gather together on an *ad hoc* basis[10] to engage in public demonstrations or protests in connection with various social and political causes. Like traditional cheerleaders, radical cheerleaders often wear short skirts and shake pompoms to generate enthusiasm among their audience, but, unlike traditional cheerleaders, they also usually display a decidedly counterculture aesthetic. Sample cheers are also available online at radcheers.tripod.com, where they are organized into such categories as girl positive, environmental, queer, and sex positive cheers. *Don't Let the System Get You Down – Cheer Up!* is a brief but entertaining and informative documentary by the New York City Radical Cheerleaders (Nedbalsky and Christmas, 2004). Included in the bonus material is a zine containing several cheers that can be printed out and distributed.

As I explain elsewhere, zines[11] are independent publications produced outside the commercial publishing process.[12] This allows zine makers, or *zinesters*, the freedom to choose content that might not otherwise make it into print. Zines are an important outlet for feminist creative work and political expression, especially among third-wave feminists.

> In many ways, third-wave feminism has emerged as a reaction by many younger feminists against the perceived rigidity and exclusivity of earlier forms of feminism. As such, it does not consist of a unified set of attitudes or beliefs. Thus, feminist zines, like the people who create them, are as likely to celebrate the experiences of sex workers as they are to condemn the sex industry as a matter of principle; they are as likely to promote political activism as they are to denounce politics altogether; and they are as likely to feature sewing patterns, recipes, and fashion advice as they are to denigrate traditional feminine roles.
>
> (Marinucci, 2006, p.375)

Culture jamming, radical cheerleading, and zine making are just three examples of queer feminist practice within popular culture. There are countless examples that I have not mentioned. Hopefully, there are also countless new examples emerging at this very moment.

Additional Resources

- Harris, L. A. (1996). 'Queer black feminism: The pleasure principle'. *Feminist Review*, 54, 3–30.
- Spivak, G. C. (1996). 'Subaltern studies: Deconstructing historiography'. In D.

Landry and G. Maclean (eds), *The Spivak Reader: Selected Works of Gayati Chakravorty Spivak*, pp.203–36. London: Routledge (original work published in 1985).
- Marinucci, M. (2006). 'Zines'. In L. Heywood (ed.), *The Women's Movement Today: An Encyclopedia of Third-Wave Feminism*, pp.374–76, Westport: Greenwood Publishing Group.
- Bullock, M. (2002). 'Interview with Naomi Klein'. *Index Magazine*. Available online at http://www.indexmagazine.com/interviews/naomi_klein.shtml
- Microcosm Publishing (2002). *The Stolen Sharpie Revolution*. Portland: Microcosm Publishing.
- Nedbalsky, J. and Christmas, M. (2004). *Don't Let the System Get You Down – Cheer Up!* Independent video documentary available online at www.nycradicalcheerleaders.org.

References

Barnard, I. (2004). *Queer Race: Cultural Interventions in the Racial Politics of Queer Theory.* New York: Peter Lang.

Baum, L. F. (2005). *15 Books in 1: L. Frank Baum's Original 'Oz' Series.* Shoes and Ships and Sealing Wax, Ltd (original works published 1908–20).

Baumgardner, J. and Richards, A. (2000). *Manifesta: Young Women, Feminism, and the Future.* New York: Farrar, Straus and Giroux.

Bullock, M. (2002). 'Interview with Naomi Klein'. *Index Magazine*. Available online at http://www.indexmagazine.com/interviews/naomi_klein.shtml

Collins, P. H. (1990). *Black Feminist Thought: Knowledge, Consciousness, and the Politics of Empowerment.* New York: Routledge.

Cruz-Malavé, A. and Manalansan, M. F. (eds). (2002). *Queer Globalizations: Citizenship and the Afterlife of Colonialism.* New York: NYU Press.

Davis, A. Y. (1981). *Women, Race, & Class.* New York: Random House.

Duncomb, S. (1997). *Notes from Underground: Zines and the Politics of Alternative Culture.* London: Verso.

Ferguson, R. A. (2004). *Aberrations in Black: Toward a Queer of Color Critique.* Minneapolis: University of Minnesota Press.

Grigg-Spall, H. (2010). 'Reproductive writes: I choose my choice: An interview with Elizabeth Kissling', *Bitch Media*, 22 March 2010. Retrieved 11 July 2010 from http://bitchmagazine.org/post/reproductive-writes-i-choose-my-choice-an-interview-with-elizabeth-kissling.

Harris, L. A. (1996). 'Queer black feminism: The pleasure principle'. *Feminist Review*, 54, 3–30.

Jagose, A. (1996). *Queer Theory: An Introduction.* New York: NYU Press.

Kamuf, P. (ed.) (1991). *A Derrida Reader.* New York: Columbia University Press.

Klein, N. (1999). *No Logo: Taking Aim at the Brand Bullies.* New York: Picador.

Lasn, K. (2000). *Culture Jam: How to Reverse America's Suicidal Consumer Binge – And Why We Must.* New York: Harper Collins.

Marinucci, M. (2006). 'Zines'. In L. Heywood (ed.), *The Women's Movement Today: An Encyclopedia of Third-Wave Feminism*, pp.374–6, Westport: Greenwood Publishing Group.

Microcosm Publishing (2002). *The Stolen Sharpie Revolution*. Portland: Microcosm Publishing.

Nedbalsky, J. and Christmas, M. (2004). *Don't Let the System Get You Down – Cheer Up!* Independent video documentary available online at www.nycradicalcheerleaders.org.

Rodriguez, J. M. (2003). *Queer Latinidad: Identity Practices, Discursive Spaces*. New York: NYU Press.

Spivak, G. C. (1996). 'Subaltern studies: Deconstructing historiography'. In D. Landry and G. Maclean (eds), *The Spivak Reader: Selected Works of Gayati Chakravorty Spivak*, pp.203–36. London: Routledge (original work published in 1985).

Walker, A. (1983). *In Search of Our Mothers' Gardens: Womanist Prose*. New York: Harcourt Brace Jovanovich.

Notes

1   Consider, for example, that in its early years, the National Organization for Women (NOW), led by Betty Friedan, blatantly excluded lesbian concerns for fear of being regarded as a lesbian organization. Friedan is rumoured to have referred to NOW's lesbian membership as the 'Lavender Menace', a title that was adopted as the name of a lesbian group that eventually formed to protest their exclusion from NOW and the mainstream feminist movement.

2   Consider, for example, that feminism has been critical of gay male drag performance for its alleged mockery of 'real' women, and also of gay male sexual intimacy for its alleged promiscuity.

3   Consider that one of the most powerful expressions of bias against any population is to deny its very existence, and it is therefore significant that there is almost no mention of bisexual women (or men, for that matter) in the canonical feminist literature.

4   There is almost no mention of transgender women and men in the canonical feminist literature. In fact, the most significant discussion of trans identity to emerge from the feminist movement centres on the exclusion of trans women from the Michigan Womyn's Music Festival, as discussed in Chapter 5.

5   These problems have been documented quite thoroughly by many different theorists. Particularly effective examples include Angela Davis (1981), Alice Walker (1983), and Patricia Hill Collins (1990).

6   For discussions at the intersection of queer theory and race theory, for example, refer to Barnard (2004) and Ferguson (2004). For a queer examination of the interconnected issues of language and ethnic identity, refer to Rodriguez (2003). For a collection of essays that explore the relationship between sexual identity and global citizenship, refer to Cruz-Malavé and Manalansan (2002). For an early, albeit brief, account that addresses the connections among queer theory and gender, race, and class, refer to Harris (1996).

7   Sexism within sexuality studies has been discussed by many people in many venues. Indeed, the exclusion of women and women's issues from the early gay rights movement is often identified as the underlying reason for the introduction of the term 'lesbian' into contemporary vernacular. For a brief summary of this history, refer, for example, to Jagose (1996), pp.44–57.

8   Racism and classism within sexuality studies are addressed, for example, in

Barnard (2004), Ferguson (2004), and Rodriguez (2003).

9 To learn more about Derrida, a good starting point is Kamuf's *A Derrida Reader* (1991).

10 A Latin expression that literally means 'for this', *ad hoc* refers to something that occurs only for a specific purpose and is often contrasted with something more permanent.

11 Note that 'zine' is pronounced exactly the way it is pronounced in the word 'magazine' from which it derives.

12 For more information, including reproductions of pages from a wide variety of different zines, refer to Duncomb (1997).

Appendix

Terms and Concepts

*'Goodness me! what a queer lot of people you are,' exclaimed the
rubber bear, looking at the assembled company.*
(L. Frank Baum, *The Road to Oz*, p.196)

This section does not supply new material, but consists instead of
passages collected from throughout the rest of the text. This section
functions much like a glossary, because it contains passages that explain
or otherwise comment on the usage of some abstract concepts and
controversial terms associated with queer theory, feminism, and related
subject matter. Unlike a conventional glossary, however, it provides more
commentary and discussion than delineation and precision. Again unlike
a conventional glossary, which arranges entries alphabetically, this section
arranges the selected terms conceptually and chronologically, presenting
them in roughly the same order in which they appear throughout the
text. The advantage of this format is twofold. First, it positions each
term within the context in which it was used in the text, thus fostering
a more richly nuanced understanding of the featured concepts than is
usually achieved through the use of decontextualized, dictionary-style
definitions. Of course, those who prefer to access the relevant passages
directly can always make use of the index at the back of the book.
The other advantage of this format is that, because the terms are listed
chapter by chapter and section by section, this appendix can be useful
for reiterating the content of individual chapters and whole sections, or
for preparing to read individual chapters and whole sections apart from
the rest of the book.

SECTION I: SEXUALITY

1: The Social Construction of Sexuality

Essentialism

Essentialism is the belief that homosexuality and other identity categories reflect innate characteristics that comprise the fundamental nature of the members of those categories. Because the essentialist account regards homosexuality as an enduring feature of the human condition, rather than the product of social contingencies, those who accept essentialism often assume that homosexuality is historically and culturally universal.

Essentialism can be and has been applied to other identity categories as well, such as those connected with concepts of gender and race. In a more abstract sense, essentialism dates at least as far back as the ancient Greek philosopher Plato, who maintained that all general terms or categories reflect universal, eternal, pure, divine archetypes. Plato referred to these archetypes as *Forms* or *Ideas*, depending on the translation. This version of essentialism is usually contrasted with nominalism, according to which the only thing that unites the disparate members of any category is the contingent social fact that they happen to be given the same name. In response to Plato, for example, the ancient Greek philosopher Aristotle claimed that reality is comprised of individuals, or *tokens*, rather than universals, or *types*.

Binary

Binary refers to a dualism or dualistic division, usually in service of some form of essentialism.

Social Constructionism

Some theorists who resist the popular assumption that the interests of lesbian women and gay men are best served by an essentialist perspective on homosexuality instead suggest that the categories associated with sexual pleasure and desire are historical and cultural developments. This thesis, often referred to as social constructionism, applies to heterosexual identity as well as alternative sexual identity categories, such as homosexual, lesbian, gay, and bisexual. This does not mean that specific sexual acts are unique to the social contexts in which they occur. A wide range of physical interactions and bodily manipulations connected with sexual desire or conducive to sexual pleasure occur across cultural and historical boundaries. The relationship of these interactions and manipulations to socially entrenched concepts of sexuality and categories of sexual identity, however, is far from universal.

Social constructionism, like essentialism, can be and has been applied to other identity categories as well, such as those connected with concepts of gender and race. In a more general sense, social constructionism is the belief that reality, as known to humans, is a product of human invention.

Semantic Holism

Thomas Kuhn maintained that the terminology employed within the various sciences is part of an interwoven web of beliefs, such that the meaning of any individual term is fully understood only by direct or indirect reference to the larger vocabulary and corresponding belief system. The indoctrination of scientists is largely a matter of language acquisition, and the language acquired determines standards of evidence and, hence, the range of empirical facts to be acknowledged and explained. This characterization is sometimes referred to as semantic holism and contrasted with semantic atomism.

Semantic Atomism

Whereas holism explains the individual parts by reference to the greater whole, atomism explains the whole by reference to its constituent parts.

Paradigm

The notion of a paradigm, as it is used here, is an extension of a concept introduced and developed by Thomas Kuhn in reference to scientific practice. Kuhn maintained that the meaning of scientific terms is dependent on the overall framework, or paradigm, in which those terms occur. Kuhn also maintained that, just as the ambiguous image is consistent with more than one interpretive framework, it is often the case that the empirical evidence is consistent with more than one paradigm.

Underdetermination

Although it is not necessarily the case that *every* theory and *every* paradigm is consistent with the empirical evidence, it is often the case that multiple theories and multiple paradigms are consistent with the empirical evidence. For this reason, evidence alone is often insufficient to determine the choice of one theory or one paradigm over another. To put it another way, theories and paradigms are often underdetermined.

Relativism

According to extreme versions of relativism, there is no relationship between reality and interpretation, and no distinction between fact and fiction. It is useful to differentiate between descriptive and prescriptive forms of relativism. While descriptive relativism amounts to the fairly uncontroversial notion that beliefs and practices vary from person to person and from culture to culture, prescriptive relativism therefore concludes that no meaningful distinction can be made between better and worse beliefs and practices. Not every reference to relativism goes to the extreme of eliminating the distinction between fact and fiction, but there is a prevalent concern that challenging notions of absolute truth and objective reality begins the descent down a slippery slope in that direction.

Pederasty

Sexual relations between older and younger men, which were commonplace in ancient Athens, are often referred to as pederasty. While pederasty refers, literally, to the love of boys, it is generally used to identify sexual relations between an adult male and a male who is younger, but past the age of puberty. Pederasty is distinguished from pedophilia, which refers to sexual relations between any adult and a prepubescent boy or girl.

Hijra

The term hijra is applied to those born male or intersex who undergo surgical castration in order to dress as women and inhabit an intermediate gender role.

Intersex

Intersex refers to people who were born with biological characteristics that do not differentiate them as clearly biologically female, nor as clearly biologically male. In many cases, intersex people are subject to medical intervention shortly after birth to facilitate a closer match between their physical presentation and a recognizably feminine or masculine gender identity.

Hermaphrodite

Historically, the term hermaphrodite was used to refer to certain forms of what is now more commonly identified as intersex. The term hermaphrodite is potentially misleading if used to refer generically to all intesex bodies. It implies the presence of both male and female genitals, but not all intersex bodies match this characterization. Although some people prefer to be identified as hermaphrodites, more people prefer the designation of intersex. Moreover, some regard hermaphrodite as outdated, insensitive, and even offensive.

Transgender

Transgender refers to people who were born as biological females but identify internally, and often socially, as men, as well as people who were born as biological males but identify internally, and often socially, as women. Some, but certainly not all, transgender men and women seek medical intervention to facilitate a closer match between their physical presentation and the identity they experience internally.

Berdache
Applied by anthropologists in reference to people who crossed gender lines in various Native American tribes, the term berdache is regarded by some Native Americans as a careless, and sometimes offensive, alternative to the use of tribal names

Lhamana
The Zuni used the term *lhamana* to refer to people who were born male and lived their adult lives as women.

Two-Spirit People
Certain people in many Native American tribes were believed be two-spirited, simultaneously female and male. They often served as healers and performed sacred rituals.

2: The Social History of Lesbian and Gay Identity

Sodomy
Today, sodomy is often used to refer specifically to anal sex, but it also refers more generally to any sexual intercourse other than when penis is received by vagina. Buggery, used primarily in England, has similar connotations.

Discourse
Foucault used the term discourse, not simply in reference to dialogue or discussion, but instead to refer more broadly to 'ways of constituting knowledge, together with the social practices, forms of subjectivity and power relations which inhere in such knowledges and relations between them' (Weedon, 1987, p.108).

Sexual Inversion
The medical community did not acknowledge female homosexuality until late 19th- and early 20th-century sexologists addressed what they referred to as 'sexual inversion', a condition believed to be characterized by the complete reversal of gender, including sexual attraction toward members of the same sex. The ideas of sex researchers Krafft-Ebing and Ellis were popularized in Radclyffe Hall's 1928 novel, *The Well of Loneliness* (Hall, 1990), for which Ellis wrote the foreword.

Gay
Gay is sometimes used, like homosexual, to refer to homosexual women as well as homosexual men. More often, however, gay is used in reference to homosexuality among men, whereas lesbian is used in reference to homosexuality among women.

Lesbian
As an alternative to the term gay, lesbian is often used in reference to homosexuality among women.

Lesbian-Baiting
Lesbian-baiting occurs when women are labelled as lesbians, not for engaging sexually with other women, but for other perceived violations of assigned gender roles. In particular, women who embody feminist principles are often characterized as lesbians. By equating feminist identity with lesbian identity, lesbian-baiting is an attempt, often successful, to capitalize on negative attitudes about homosexuality to prevent women from identifying as feminists.

3: Queer Alternatives

Revolutionary Practice
The term practice is used here, not in reference to repetition or rehearsal, but rather to patterns of social behaviour and interaction. Karl Marx, for example, described practice as 'sensuous human activity' (1970, p.121) and remarked that 'coincidence of the changing of circumstances and of human activity or self-changing can be conceived and rationally understood only as *revolutionary practice*' (1970, p.121).

Paradigm Change
Just as Marx made reference to revolutionary practice, Kuhn made reference to revolutionary science. For Kuhn, normal scientific practice, characterized by consensus around an established paradigm, is contrasted with revolutionary scientific practice, characterized by crisis and conflict.

A parallel exists between paradigm change, or revolution, in the context of scientific practice and paradigm change, or revolution, in the larger context of political practice. In scientific practice and in political practice, crisis, along with a corresponding potential for revolution, occurs when the established paradigm ceases to accommodate the world it helped to create.

In the context of science, Kuhn noted, there 'are always difficulties somewhere in the paradigm-nature fit', but these are usually resolved in the course of normal scientific practice (1970, p.82). The fit between paradigm and nature, or between theories and facts, is never perfect, and much of normal scientific practice consists of what Kuhn referred to as the 'mopping-up operations' (1970, p.24) of extending and articulating the accepted paradigm. Not all messes are easily mopped up, however, and not all mismatches between paradigm and nature are easily reconciled. When an especially stubborn mismatch between paradigm and nature 'comes to seem more than just another puzzle of normal science', according to Kuhn, 'the transition to crisis and to extraordinary science has begun' (1970, p.82).

The Homophile Movement

Homosexual men began to form homophile organizations in Europe 'in the same period in which homosexuality crystallized as an identity, when for the first time it was possible to *be* a homosexual' (Jagose, 1996, p.22). These organizations upheld the rights of homosexuals by noting the consensus within the medical community around the notion of homosexuality as a congenital condition (Jagose, 1996, p.22).

The Gay Liberation Movement

Some resented the clinical connotations of the term homosexual along with the apologetic attitude (Jagose, 1996, p.27) of the homophile movement. Gay identity thus emerged as an alternative to homosexual identity, and the gay liberation movement emerged as an alternative to the homophile movement.

Although it is an oversimplification, the Stonewall riots of 1969 are often cited as the beginning of the gay liberation movement. The Stonewall Inn was a New York gay and drag bar, predominately Black and Latino, and it was subject, like many gay bars at the time, to occasional police raids. These raids usually resulted in arrests for such forms of 'indecency' as dancing, kissing, and cross dressing. When Stonewall was raided in the early morning hours of 28 June 1969, however, the patrons fought back, and they continued fighting all weekend. This sudden and unanimous expression of outrage is sometimes attributed to the death of gay icon Judy Garland, whose funeral was held on 27 June 1969, but a more likely explanation is that these riots, as well as the gay liberation movement and other movements of the same era, including the women's liberation movement and the Black civil rights movement, were evidence of a growing sense of injustice in response to discrimination.

The LGBT Movement

Although gay can be used in reference to women as well as men, the gay liberation movement was concerned primarily with gay men, and many lesbian women wanted the movement to recognize and include lesbian identity more explicitly. As a result of this demand, homosexual identity is usually referred to in terms of both lesbian identity and gay male identity. Unlike references to gay identity, which could include lesbian women, references to gay men and lesbian women are explicitly inclusive.

While more inclusive than gay, references to gay and lesbian identity do not reflect the full range of alternatives to heterosexuality. Given the popular misconception that bisexuality is a temporary identity that people eventually overcome, either by fully committing to homosexuality or by fully committing to heterosexuality, it is especially important to assert bisexuality as a sexual identity distinct from both heterosexuality and homosexuality. In order to encompass a broader range of identities and issues, references to alternative sexualities were expanded to include bisexual identity. A drawback of this expanded terminology is that it is longer and somewhat more awkward than referring to gay, or even gay and lesbian, identities. For this reason, the abbreviation GLB was introduced to refer to gay, lesbian, and bisexual identities. Recognizing that women always seem to come second, some people preferred to rearrange the order the letters LGB, symbolically putting women ahead of men.

The recent addition of transgender identity completes a now familiar list, GLBT or LGBT. Unlike lesbian, gay, and bisexual, the category of transgender does not address sexual partner choice. Instead, it addresses the discrepancy some people experience between the biological sex category to which they were assigned and their identification as women or men. The inclusion of transgender people when accounting for alternative sexualities is not altogether arbitrary, however. Many who identify as lesbian, gay, or bisexual experience discrimination and violence for deviating from the heterosexual norm, and this is also the case for those who identify as transgender. Lesbian, gay, bisexual, and transgender identities all challenge the widespread expectation that biological females and biological males should exhibit the specific collection of attitudes and behaviours assigned to each sex category, and that they should partner sexually only with biological members of the opposite sex and corresponding gender categories.

Gender
Although the concepts of gender, sex, and sexuality are interrelated, it is often useful to differentiate among them. Gender usually refers to constellations of characteristics commonly regarded as feminine and masculine. While sex is generally believed to be biologically innate, gender is generally believed to be socially acquired.

Sex
Although the concepts of gender, sex, and sexuality are interrelated, it is often useful to differentiate among them. Sex usually refers to constellations of characteristics commonly regarded as female and male. While gender is generally believed to be socially acquired, sex is generally believed to be biologically innate.

Sexuality
Although the concepts of gender, sex, and sexuality are interrelated, it is often useful to differentiate among them. Sexuality usually refers to

intimate practices, especially those related to the selection of intimate partners, and there is widespread disagreement about whether sexuality is socially acquired or biologically innate.

Queer Theory

In a thoroughly revolutionary alternative to the established paradigm, queer theory avoids binary and hierarchical reasoning in general, and in connection with gender, sex, and sexuality in particular. This is part of the reason queer theory is notoriously difficult to define. In philosophy, a successful definition is often understood as an articulation of the necessary and sufficient conditions under which the term to be defined may be meaningfully and accurately applied. In other words, it draws an unproblematic boundary between the members of a given category and everything else, thereby participating in binary reasoning rather than transcending it. Queer theory, which trades essentialism and semantic atomism for social constructionism and semantic holism, recognizes that meaning is conveyed not by definitions of individual terms but by contextual relations between and among various terms. According to Jagose, 'Broadly speaking, queer describes those gestures or analytical models which dramatize incoherencies in the allegedly stable relations between chromosomal sex, gender and sexual desire' (Jagose, 1996, p.3). Although this is not a definition in the customary sense, it is an informative description nonetheless. Those already familiar with postmodernism might also benefit from the overly simplified but potentially explanatory description of queer theory as a postmodern interpretation of gender, sex, and sexuality.

SECTION II: SEX

4: Unwelcome Interventions

Genderfucking

Given that biological criteria for determining sex are not publicly accessible and secondary sex characteristics are not always reliable, it is remarkable that there is not more confusion when it comes to separating people on the basis of sex. The ease with which most people can be recognized as female or male has less to do with their biology than it has to do with various social markers. Although anyone, female or male, can wear a dress or a short hairstyle, such social displays are fairly reliable unless people consciously present themselves in an ambiguous manner, which is sometimes referred to informally as genderfucking

The Twins Case

Bruce Reimer, who was identified at birth as biologically male, was surgically reassigned as female following a botched circumcision. Bruce was renamed Brenda and raised as a girl. Bruce's identical twin brother, Brian, suffered no complications and was raised as a boy. Because the two children were identical twins, this case was regarded by many as an opportunity to empirically test the theory that the distinction between women and men is primarily attributable to socialization. Initially, Brenda's reassignment was believed to be so successful that the 'twins case' was cited in many women's studies textbooks as evidence of gender socialization. Apparently, however, Brenda never felt completely comfortable as a girl and eventually resumed a male identity, this time under the name David Reimer. Sadly, Reimer never found peace and finally committed suicide in 2004.

5: Welcome Transformations

Michfest
In 1976, sisters Linda and Kristie Vogel, along with their friend Mary Kindig, organized a summer concert in Hart, Michigan, featuring music by and for women. The concert was so successful that it became an annual event, now known as the Michigan Womyn's Music Festival, or less formally, 'Michfest' or even just 'Michigan', and abbreviated throughout as MWMF. As indicated in a promotional flyer from 1978, the festival was conceived as 'A Gathering of Mothers and Daughters for Womyn-Born Womyn' (Vogel, 2000). According to Linda Vogel, 'The hallmark of Michigan has always been its creation of separate, self-defined and deeply honored womyn's space' (Vogel, 2000). The festival grounds, often referred to simply as 'the land', are designated exclusively for women, which reflects a commitment to the separatist agenda associated with some versions of radical feminism.

Womyn
'Womyn' is sometimes used instead of 'wo*men*' and 'womon' is used instead of 'wo*man*' as an alternative to the use of terminology that is referential of men and masculinity.

Camp Trans
The women-born-women requirement excluded trans women, and outrage over this exclusion led to the creation of Camp Trans. Initially conceived as a protest site following Nancy Burkholder's 1991 eviction from the festival grounds, Camp Trans waned within a few years, but re-emerged in 1999 as an alternative festival venue existing alongside MWMF, offering workshops on and gaining support for trans inclusion.

Gender Identity Disorder
While many trans activists advocated for the inclusion of gender identity disorder (GID) as a psychological disorder in the 1980 update of the *Diagnostic and Statistical Manual of Mental Disorders* (DSM-III), many feminists repudiate GID for attempting to establish meaningful distinctions between appropriate and inappropriate forms of gender expression. It is worth noting that although many trans activists favour the continued use of GID as a medical diagnosis, the many who do not are working diligently in an effort to have it removed from the next updated edition of the DSM. Additionally, trans people who favour the continued inclusion of GID in the DSM often do so for pragmatic reasons, such as easier access to prescribed treatments, primarily hormone therapy and sex reassignment surgery. Feminists who do not identify as trans are often slow to recognize the significance of such practical considerations, and comparatively quick to express objections based on principle.

FTM
The abbreviation FTM is sometimes used to make quick and easy reference to female-to-male transgender people, or trans men.

MTF
The abbreviation MTF is sometimes used to make quick and easy reference to male-to-female transgender people, or trans women.

Butch
Butch is often used in reference to some women, including some lesbian women, who exhibit a traditionally masculine personal style without identifying as male. In other words, butch women (or simply, butches) do not identify as transgender. Butch identity is sometimes contrasted with the traditionally feminine style of femme women (or simply, femmes).

Packing
Packing refers to the practice among some trans men, and even some butch women, of wearing a dildo or other prosthetic under the clothing in order to approximate the bodily presence of a penis.

Cisgender
The term cisgender was introduced as a way to refer to those who are not transgender without resorting to words like 'biological' or 'regular', which inevitably imply that the gender expression of people who do not identify as transgender is more authentic than or otherwise preferable to the gender expression of people who do identify as transgender. According to some people, however, cisgender is a problematic, perhaps even self-defeating, term because it can be interpreted as suggesting that those who identify as lesbian, gay, or bisexual, for example, but not as

transgender, experience no mismatch between their own gender identity and gender expression and cultural expectations regarding gender identity and expression.

Genderqueer

The term genderqueer is used to refer to all manner of identities and sexualities that expose the 'mismatches between sex, gender and sexual desire' (Jagose, 1996, p.3) for those who are unwilling or unable to define themselves in terms of the established binary.

SECTION III: GENDER

6: Gender Defined and Undefined

Existentialism

Existentialism usually refers to a philosophical school of thought associated with Jean-Paul Sartre, Simone de Beauvoir, and many others, particularly during the first half of the 20th century. Although there is a great deal of variation from one theorist to the next, a common thread running through the different perspectives is the search for meaning in a causally determined physical world.

Alterity

The dominant group is defined by whom it excludes, and not merely by whom it includes. The identification of someone or something as different from oneself is often referred to as *alterity*.

The Other

As an existentialist, Beauvoir was concerned about the tension between freedom and determinism and believed that there is nothing necessary or inevitable about who a person ultimately becomes. Applied to the distinction between women and men, this means that one must become a woman in order to be a woman. The process of becoming a woman is intimately intertwined with the process by which someone is identified as or differentiated from a man. The male self is asserted as the subject, or the 'One' only by identifying the female as the object, or the 'Other'.

This explanation of how people come to identify as women and men suggests that these identity categories are contingent. To regard them as contingent is to acknowledge that they could have been, and perhaps could yet be, other than they are. By recognizing that 'no subset of human beings is destined by biology or a distinctive essence to being the absolute Other' (Frye, 1996, p.994), Beauvoir anticipated what would eventually be identified as the sex-gender distinction.

Gender-Neutral Language
Language is neutral when a single term is used to refer equally to all of the different categories of people.

Gender-Inclusive Language
Language is inclusive when multiple terms are used to refer separately and specifically to more than one, and ideally to all, relevant categories of people.

Hegemony
The term hegemony refers to power, particularly of a state, that exerts a controlling influence over others.

Hegemonic Binary
Binary refers to a dualism or dualistic division, usually in service of some form of essentialism. In service of a deeply essentialist account of gender, sex, and sexuality, the hegemonic binary refers to the coalescence of gender, sex, and sexuality into exactly two fundamentally distinct natural kinds: women and men.

Natural Kinds
The traditional doctrine of natural kinds reflects an underlying commitment to essentialism about the natural world. According to John Dupré (1993), there are three conditions that must be met according to essentialist versions of the doctrine of natural kinds: first, natural kind categories should be clearly and unambiguously delineated. Second, natural kind categories should be a product of discovery rather than invention or creation. Third, natural kind categories should reveal as much information as possible about the members of those categories – and, ideally, they will reveal *all* of the essential characteristics of those members (Dupré, 1993, pp.17–18). The traditional, essentialist, doctrine of natural kinds depicts an orderly world that divides into thoroughly informative categories inclusive of all phenomena without leftovers or crossovers.

Hilary Kornblith represents natural kinds as 'homeostatic property clusters' in which underlying structures produce the observable properties that are distinctive of various natural kinds (Kornblith, 1993). Kornblith suggests that experience reveals which properties and which sorts of properties are indicative of relevant underlying structural differences.

Platonic Forms
The theory of the Forms is addressed in many of Plato's works, but the allegory of the prisoners in the cave in Book VII of the *The Republic* offers a particularly vivid exposition (Plato, 1991, pp.253–61). The allegory of the cave describes a group of prisoners chained up in such a

way that they can see only shadows on the cave wall in front of them. The shadows are produced by physical objects placed before the fire behind them. An analogy is drawn between these imperfect shadows and the imperfection of the physical world. Just as physical objects are more real and more perfect than mere shadows, so too are the Forms more real and more perfect than any of the particular things encountered in the everyday world. Unlike the particulars that populate the everyday world, Forms are perfect, eternal, universal abstractions, much like the concepts or categories of which the various particular things are members.

Performativity

Borrowing from the example of drag performance, Butler indicates that, unlike the imitation of the Forms, the imitation that occurs in drag, or any other performance of gender, is an imitation that has no original. There is not something real that gender imitates. What gender imitates is simply other performances of gender, which are themselves mere imitations. Butler remarks that '*gender is a kind of imitation for which there is no original*; in fact, it is a kind of imitation that produces the very notion of the original as an effect and consequence of the imitation itself' (Butler, 1993, p.313).

Queering

Instead of attempting to repair the language and meaning surrounding existing categories of gender, sex, and sexuality, there is also the option, as expressed in the title of Butler's 1990 book, of making 'Gender Trouble'. Making gender trouble simply means directing attention toward rather than away from the limitations of existing categories, particularly the existing categories of gender, sex, and sexuality associated with the hegemonic binary. Thus, rather than attempting to resolve the dispute regarding gender-neutral language and gender-inclusive language, a meaningful third option is to use the problematic existing terminology, particularly when doing so is most likely to emphasize mismatches within the categories of gender, sex, and sexuality associated with the hegemonic binary. This can also be characterized as a 'queering' of the established binaries. As explained by Anamarie Jagose, 'queer' refers to 'those gestures or analytical models which dramatize incoherencies in the allegedly stable relations between chromosomal sex, gender and sexual desire' (Jagose, 1996, p.3). To disrupt the hegemonic binary, perhaps even in very small ways, serves to 'queer' the paradigm. Making 'Gender Trouble', rather than attempting to resolve or eliminate such trouble, is thus a viable alternative for dealing with the existence of the sorts of incoherencies that Jagose seems to have in mind.

7: Feminism Examined and Explored

The First Wave

Feminism as a social and political movement, particularly within the USA, is often represented with the metaphor of waves that swell and retreat depending on the level of enthusiasm and need for feminist intervention. The first wave of the women's movement is usually associated with the suffrage movement that culminated in the passage of the 19th amendment giving US women the legal right to vote in 1920.

The Second Wave

Feminism as a social and political movement, particularly within the USA, is often represented with the metaphor of waves that swell and retreat depending on the level of enthusiasm and need for feminist intervention. The second wave of the women's movement is associated with what is often referred to as the women's liberation movement, which led to a number of legal and social developments, including an increase in women in the paid workforce and increased attention to the problem of violence against women.

The Third Wave

Feminism as a social and political movement, particularly within the USA, is often represented with the metaphor of waves that swell and retreat depending on the level of enthusiasm and need for feminist intervention. Although there is some disagreement about whether or not the second wave is over, those who believe that a third wave has begun often associate it with pluralism and the celebration of variation among people in general, and among women in particular.

Phallocentrism

Phallocentrism refers to a bias that favours men.

Gynocentrism

Gynocentrism refers to the adoption, often intentionally, of a bias that favours women.

Feminist Theory

Feminist theory refers to theorizing that addresses feminist questions and concerns.

Liberal Feminism

Rooted in political liberalism, liberal feminism presupposes a universal rationality such that good, careful reasoning is all that is needed in order to establish social justice. Like political liberalism, liberal feminism denies that accident of birth is sufficient to justify an inequitable distribution of good, including such intangible goods as rights and opportunities. By rejecting the notion that nature warrants the subordinate status of women, liberal feminism gives birth to the distinction between sex and gender. According to liberal feminism, sexism is the product of bad reasoning, and the goal of feminism is to make the necessary corrections, particularly within the legal system.

Womanism
Alice Walker articulated womanism as alternative to the white, sometimes even racist, orientation of mainstream feminism. Womanism shares with liberal feminism an interest in liberation strategies. The difference, however, is that womanism, unlike liberal feminism, addresses intersectionality.

Intersectionality
Intersectionality refers to the simultaneous impact of race, gender, and class on the lives of Black women (Davis, 1981; Crenshaw, 1994).

Marxist Feminism
Dissatisfaction with liberal feminism invites an analysis of the structural constraints contributing to the subordination of women, particularly capitalism. Just as Marxism identifies capitalism as the source of oppression, Marxist feminism (for example Reed, 1970) identifies capitalism as the source of women's oppression. On this account, the role of women within contemporary western society is rooted not in biology but in the rise of capitalism. From this perspective, the remedy is obvious. Although women have traditionally done most of the domestic labour, this labour goes unacknowledged by a social system that presupposed the economic dependence of women on men. Women need power, which derives from economic leverage. Marxist feminism therefore advocates the socialization of domestic labour or the more thorough integration of women into the wage labour system.

Radical Feminism
Marxist feminism has been criticized for reducing women's oppression to a subcategory of economic oppression. In a now famous analysis of rape, Catharine MacKinnon (1987) addresses the limitations of both liberal and Marxist approaches to feminism. On an economic model, rape is construed as an issue of property rights. Sex becomes rape only when it occurs as an act of wrongful possession between a man and a woman to whom he is not sexually entitled. The legal distinction between rape and consensual sex, according to MacKinnon, fosters this interpretation. It reinforces the role of men as those who seek a commodity, namely sex, that is owned by women (or their fathers, husbands, brothers, and other protectors). MacKinnon claims that, by differentiating between sex and

rape, some feminist analyses inadvertently perpetuate a system of sexual violence against women. For this reason, MacKinnon adopts radical feminism and advocates voluntary lesbianism as an alternative to the power symmetry inherent in heterosexual relationships.

Adrienne Rich also advocates voluntary lesbianism, which is used almost interchangeably with woman-identification, as an alternative to the oppressive system that enforces the heterosexual norm. While not all radical feminists oppose heterosexuality, they do tend to agree that it is historically and socially problematic (for example Bunch, 1975; Rich, 1980). This is because heterosexual relationships often perpetuate *patriarchy*. Various articulations of radical feminism are unified by their mutual critique of patriarchy as the fundamental source of sexism.

Patriarchy
Patriarchy is best characterized as a social structure that grants priority to that which is male or masculine over that which is female or feminine.

Socialist Feminism
Socialist feminism emerges as something of a synthesis of Marxist and radical feminisms. Socialist feminism opposes the primacy of class in Marxist analyses and of sex in radical analyses, and instead regards capitalism and male sexual dominance as equal partners in the subordination of women (for example Hartmann, 1981). For this reason, it is believed that socialist reform is necessary, but that reform efforts will be adequate only if they address the often hidden female half of the labour force. According to socialist feminism, lower classes of men are simultaneously privileged and disadvantaged. They possess power in relation to women, but they lack power in the larger social context. Since men have no immediate or obvious interest in relinquishing power over women, socialist reform will be insufficient unless it is also feminist.

Multicultural Feminism
Multicultural and global feminisms both exhibit interest in, and respect for, the lived experiences of women who are outside the dominant white culture. Multicultural feminism (for example Collins, 1990; Anzaldua, 1987), also sometimes referred to as 'women of color feminism', addresses the unique issues that racial and ethnic minority women experience as a result of the intersecting influences of gender, race, class, and sexuality on cultural identities.

Global Feminism
Multicultural and global feminisms both exhibit interest in, and respect for, the lived experiences of women who are outside the mainstream culture of white Americans and Europeans. Global feminism (for example

Mies, 1986; Enloe, 1995) represents a broader perspective which regards the lives of all women as inextricably interconnected, regardless of their geographic and political separation. In particular, global feminism examines the impact of imperialism and colonialism, thereby bringing international politics to the analysis of women's issues. Consider, for instance, Cynthia Enloe's (1995) influential article 'The Globetrotting Sneaker', which exposed the impact on people in general, but particularly on women and their children, when multinational corporations like Nike exploit the workers and natural resources in vulnerable parts of the world.

Feminist Ethics
Feminist theory refers to theorizing that addresses feminist questions and concerns. A closely related sort of theorizing that is also relevant to the present discussion is feminist philosophy, whereby a feminist perspective, attitude, or orientation is applied to philosophical questions and concerns. An example is feminist ethics, in which a feminist perspective is applied to the study of morality.

Ethics of Care
In the early 1980s, research by Carol Gilligan (1982), Nel Noddings (1984), and others suggested that girls and women may be disposed toward a different style of ethical reasoning than boys and men. Specifically, they suggested that ethics based on the natural impulse to care for others provides a feminine and feminist alternative to more familiar systems of ethics that are based on notions of justice. The ethics of care offers an alternative account in which morality is situated in relationships as a whole, rather than in discreet choices and actions or the moral rules that govern those choices and actions.

Ecofeminism
Ecofeminism resists the temptation to supply universal moral rules, and is directed instead toward revealing and addressing what Karen Warren (2000) refers to as 'the logic of domination' in the relationships between people or groups of people, and also in the relationships between people or groups of people and other parts of the natural world. The ecofeminist critique of the logic of domination is ultimately a critique of the western philosophical tradition, which has devoted itself to establishing the superiority of reason, and hence of humankind, in the specific form of mankind, over everything else.

Feminist Epistemology
Feminist theory refers to theorizing that addresses feminist questions and concerns. A closely related sort of theorizing that is also relevant to the present discussion is feminist philosophy, whereby a feminist

perspective, attitude, or orientation is applied to philosophical questions and concerns. An example is feminist epistemology, in which a feminist perspective is applied to the study of knowledge.

Logical Empiricism

Logical empiricism, sometimes referred to as logical positivism, describes the union of positivism, or empiricism, and logic. Positivism is the belief that statements are meaningful only if they are verifiable through experience. Logic is a system for analysing the formal relationships between and among statements. Logical empiricism thus refers to an account whereby knowledge, especially scientific knowledge, is produced when empirically verifiable data, in the form of observation statements, are subjected to logical analysis in order to confirm or disconfirm a range of theories and hypotheses. This account presupposes that it is both possible and desirable for scientists and other epistemic agents to be neutral in the collection and evaluation of data, such that a given epistemic agent is, or at least should be, virtually interchangeable with any other epistemic agent.

Feminist Empiricism

Feminist empiricism shares with logical empiricism a commitment to scientific neutrality, but denies that sexism and other forms of bias are easily avoided. Feminist empiricists have exposed numerous cases in which predominantly male scientific communities have misrepresented or ignored women and, as result, have generated faulty conclusions. For instance, the exclusive use of male subjects in experiments intended for generalization to the larger human population is no longer deemed acceptable, largely because feminist empiricists have revealed the hidden biases of this practice. Indeed, the ethics of care emerged as an alternative traditional ethics precisely because feminist research on moral development in children revealed that earlier work had concentrated almost exclusively on boys. According to feminist empiricism, sexist science occurs when scientists fail to reason as carefully and neutrally as they should. Thus, the role of feminist empiricism is largely corrective.

Feminist Standpoint Theory

Standpoint theory borrows from Marxism the suggestion that those living under conditions of domination have a more complete perspective than their oppressors (Smith, 1987, pp.78–88). On this account, epistemic communities consist of a dominant group, or centre, and a dominated group, or margin. From the margin, someone gains an outsider's perspective on the centre, and is thereby better equipped to expose the limitations of the dominant ideology.

Like feminist empiricism, the role of standpoint theory is largely corrective. Again like feminist empiricism, standpoint theory implies that some perspectives are epistemologically preferable to others. Unlike feminist empiricism, however, standpoint theory indicates that the corrective, privileged perspective can be achieved only from the social margins (hooks, 2000).

Modernism

In everyday usage, modern refers literally to whatever is new, whatever is happening at the current moment. In its more technical usage, modernism refers to specific eras and schools of thought within a variety of different domains, such as philosophy, science studies, art history, literary criticism, film theory, and so on. What modernism means for science studies, for example, may have very little in common with what it means for art history or any other field. Addressing very briefly its usage in philosophy, the modern era began around the beginning of the 17th century, against the historical backdrop of the scientific revolution, and lasted into the beginning of the 19th century, in the context of the Enlightenment. The Enlightenment is perhaps best described as a general attitude of celebration and optimism about the potential use of reason to obtain truth and achieve the highest human potential.

Postmodernism

Postmodernism leaves behind the optimism associated with modernism and the Enlightenment. For postmodernism in general, and for postmodern feminism in particular, there is no absolute truth. Any attempt to distinguish fact from fiction is thus a political project, based as much in ideology and values as it is in evidence and logic.

Postmodern Feminism

Like standpoint theories, postmodern feminism acknowledges that social positioning influences epistemological perspective. For postmodern feminism, in which postmodernism is applied to the subject matter of feminism, this means that there is no underlying truth about sex or gender. In a particularly provocative statement of this position, Judith Butler has suggested not just that gender is socially constructed, but that sex itself is also socially constructed. Sex, Butler claims, 'is an ideal construct which is forcibly materialized through time. It is not a simple fact or static condition of a body, but a process whereby regulatory norms materialize "sex" and achieve this materialization through a forcible reiteration of those norms' (Butler, 1993, pp.1–2).

Third-Wave Feminism

Third-wave feminism describes the newest generations of feminists at a time in history when many have suggested that, at least for women in most of Europe and North America, feminism is no longer necessary. In fact, when Rebecca Walker first made reference to the 'third-wave' in

1992, it was in response to the suggestion in a *New York Times* article that a post-feminist era was underway (Baumgardner and Richards, 2000, p.77). While some challenge the notion of third-wave feminism by suggesting that the second wave was so successful that sexism is no longer a significant problem, others challenge the notion of third-wave feminism by suggesting that the second wave has not yet completed its work.

Third-wave feminism is not easily defined, partly because it is still in the process of establishing itself, and partly because one of the features common across different articulations of third-wave feminism is its recognition that there are multiple versions of what it means to be a feminist, or even a third-wave feminism.

SECTION IV: QUEER FEMINISM

8: Notes Toward a Queer Feminism

Queer Feminism
Queer feminism is simply the application of queer notions of gender, sex, and sexuality to the subject matter of feminist theory, and the simultaneous application of feminist notions of gender, sex, and sexuality to the subject matter of queer theory. Although the word queer is commonly associated with sex and sexuality, queer theory is a way of understanding not just sex and sexuality but also gender. Specifically, queer theory avoids the binary and hierarchical reasoning usually associated with these concepts. Precisely what it is that constitutes the subject matter of feminism varies from one form of feminism to the next. Despite this diversity, however, almost every form of feminism addresses at least gender and sex, and sometimes sexuality as well. There is thus an implicit connection between queer theory and feminist theory, and queer feminism makes this connection more explicit.

Queer feminism brings both a queer orientation to feminist theory, and a feminist orientation to queer theory. Part of what makes the union of queer and feminist theory so inviting is that they already have much in common. Both address the intersecting issues of gender, sex, and sexuality. In the case of queer theory, however, the emphasis is on sex and sexuality. In the case of feminist theory, the emphasis is on gender and sex. An obvious outcome of uniting queer and feminist theory, then, is that the addition of a queer perspective promises to direct increased attention toward sexuality in the context of feminist theory, while the addition of a feminist perspective promises to direct increased attention to gender in the context of queer theory.

Strategic Essentialism

What Gayatri Spivak (1996) refers to as 'strategic essentialism' is a strategy whereby groups with mutual goals and interests temporarily present themselves publicly as essentially the same for the sake of expediency and presenting a united front, while simultaneously engaging in ongoing and less public disagreement and debate.

Index